THE CHAMPIONS LEAGUE CLASSIC KITS

The UEFA Champions League is the pinnacle of domestic football. Over the years it has hosted some of the most talented footballers in iconic club strips. Far from being just an afterthought, football kits tell the story of the club that season and are an essential sartorial decision for both teams and the millions of supporters who purchase them. Many of the kits go on to have their own moment in the spotlight and are just as recognisable as the talented footballers who wear them.

Champions League Classic Kits delves into the history, meaning and reception of these iconic outfits and the best footballing moments that took place in them. The most famous clubs from across Europe are featured, including Real Madrid, AC Milan, Bayern Munich and Barcelona, as well as Britain's winning teams, as we look at the kits worn by Liverpool, Manchester United, Chelsea, Nottingham Forest, Aston Villa and Celtic. Fully illustrated, and with in-depth discussion of sensational Champions League campaigns and statistics, this is essential reading for all lovers of the beautiful game.

ASPEN BOOKS

Please note that for formatting purposes, Most Appearances/Goals stats have been simplified to feature the players of most relevance to each season.

CONTENTS

Page	Entry
4	1966-67 Celtic
8	1979-80 Nottingham Forest
12	1981-82 Aston Villa
16	1982-83 Hamburg
20	1988-89 AC Milan
24	1990-91 Napoli
28	1991-92 Sampdoria
32	1992-93 Marseille
36	1994-95 Ajax
40	1995-96 Juventus
44	1996-97 Borussia Dortmund
48	1998-99 Manchester United
52	2000-01 Valencia
56	2001-02 Real Madrid
60	2002-03 Roma
64	2003-04 Porto
68	2004-05 Liverpool
72	2005-06 Barcelona
76	2007-08 Benfica
80	2009-10 Inter Milan
84	2011-12 Chelsea
88	2012-13 Bayern Munich
92	2015-16 Atletico Madrid
96	2017-18 Feyenoord
100	2018-19 PSV Eindhoven
104	2019-20 Paris Saint-Germain
108	2021-22 Sheriff Tiraspol

CELTIC 1966-67 HOME

Celtic became the first British club to win the main prize in European football and they did it in real style. The club had been wearing their famous green and white hooped shirts since 1903, with the version worn in the final against Inter Milan featuring a simple crew neck collar but no crest. The shorts included large numbers on the left thigh and, like the socks, were plain white. Goalkeeper Ronnie Simpson wore a traditional plain green top.

CELTIC 1966-67 HOME

This was the most successful season in Celtic's history. Not only did they retain their domestic league title by three points ahead of fierce rivals Rangers, they also won both major cup competitions in Scotland and the Glasgow Cup for good measure. It was the Bhoys' success on the continent that is best remembered though, when having twice reached the UEFA Cup Winners' Cup semi-finals in previous seasons, they entered the 1966-67 European Cup and won it at the first attempt.

After easing past Zurich and Nantes in the early rounds, Celtic came up against the reigning Yugoslav First League champions Vojvodina in the quarter-finals and for a long time seemed to be heading out of the competition. Leading 1-0 after the first match in Novi Sad, the Serbs were welcomed into Scotland by nearly 70,000 spectators at Celtic Park and the fervent home crowd had to wait until almost the hour mark before seeing their side pull level. Stevie Chalmers got the equaliser before captain Billy McNeill struck in the dying moments on a memorable Glasgow night.

The semi-final was a little more straightforward, a comfortable 3-1 win over Dukla Prague in the first leg being enough to book Celtic's place in the final. This was the 12th iteration of the showpiece event and the first time it did not feature one of the two giants of the early years of the competition, Real Madrid or Benfica. It was at least played in the Portuguese capital though, leading to Jock Stein's side being nicknamed the 'Lisbon Lions'.

Famed for the side all coming from a 30-mile radius of Celtic Park, the all-conquering Hoops had to dig deep against Internazionale, who went into the game as favourites and had already won the cup twice before in 1964 and 1965. The Italians prided themselves on a tight defence and after taking an early lead through Sandro Mazzola's penalty seemed happy to sit back – it took an excellent long range shot from Tommy Gemmell to finally beat an inspired Giuliano Sarti in the Inter goal, and when Chalmers directed the ball past him again in the final minutes Celtic's more positive approach proved worthwhile.

Inter had only conceded three goals en route to the final and had eliminated holders Real Madrid along the way, but it was Celtic that could now claim to be the best team in Europe.

CELTIC 1966-67

WINNERS
Scottish Division One

WINNERS
Scottish Cup

WINNERS
Scottish League Cup

WINNERS
European Cup

EUROPEAN CUP IN NUMBERS

61 GAMES

192 GOALS

MOST APPEARANCES
SANDRO MAZZOLA (10)
Inter Milan

TOP SCORER
PAUL VAN HIMST (6)
Anderlecht

MOST GOALS
CELTIC (18)

MOST CLEAN SHEETS
INTER MILAN (6)

10 Anderlecht put ten goals past their Finnish counterparts Haka in their first round first leg match and eventually won 12-1 on aggregate. 1860 Munich also beat Omonia 10-1 over two games.

54 CSKA Red Flag reached the semi-finals after beating Linfield 3-2, their 1-0 win in the quarter-final second leg coming courtesy of a Dimitar Yakimov strike in the 54th minute.

1966-67 European Cup Final | 25 May 1967, Lisbon

CELTIC 2-1 INTER MILAN

T. Gemmell 63'
S. Chalmers 84'

S. Mazzola 7' (pen)

NOTTINGHAM FOREST 1979-80 HOME

There was a sense of déjà vu when Nottingham Forest retained the European Cup in 1980 wearing a very similar kit to the one they used a year before. Both designs were from sportswear giant adidas and featured the company's famous three stripe trim on the sides, with the new version now including a deeper v-neck collar than before and matching sleeve cuffs. Due to colour clashes, red shorts had to be used in both finals, instead of Forest's traditional white.

Hamburg reached the final for the first time but, having eliminated giants Real Madrid, they had to face the reigning champions Nottingham Forest to decide who would take the trophy. Forest too had needed to overcome one of the competition's most decorated sides, but after beating Ajax in the semi-finals, they were ready to defend their crown at the Santiago Bernabéu Stadium – a prospect that could have been entirely different had tenants Real overcome the West German champions.

Whilst 'Los Blancos' had history on their side, their opponents in the semis could boast about having the current Ballon d'Or holder in theirs. With Kevin Keegan pulling the strings, Hamburg romped through the first four stages with a total of 19 goals, two of which came at Hajduk Split to confirm progress from the quarter-finals on away goals, and the last five coming in a memorable semi-final second leg.

For Forest, the key to success was continuity. Eight of the starting XI from the previous final against Malmo were on duty again against Hamburg, whilst six players featured in every game of their tournament run. One of the few changes had seen Frank Gray replace the retired Frank Clark in a solid defensive unit that only conceded five times in the competition, including tricky assignments against Osters of Sweden, Arges Pitesti of Romania and BFC Dynamo of East Germany in the opening rounds.

The modified back line continued to hold firm in the final to secure a narrow win, and the victory was fully deserved – the Reds did have to thank goalkeeper Peter Shilton for some fine work, but after going ahead through John Robertson's pin-point finish in the first half the team worked hard to keep their opponents' chances down to a minimum. Forest had already won the European Super Cup against Barcelona at the Camp Nou three months earlier and now they had completed an impressive double on Spanish soil.

As well as the European Cup, the club were a fraction away from retaining another trophy in the 1979-80 campaign. League Cup holders for the last two seasons and successful against their great rivals of the time Liverpool in the semi-finals, Forest eventually lost the final to underdogs Wolverhampton Wanderers by a single goal. The match was a close run thing, but it was their success on the continent that had done most to secure boss Brian Clough's place amongst the elite of football management.

NOTTINGHAM FOREST 1979-80

5TH PLACE
English Division One

4TH ROUND
English FA Cup

RUNNERS-UP
English League Cup

WINNERS
European Cup

 BRIAN CLOUGH

JOHN ROBERTSON

EUROPEAN CUP IN NUMBERS

61 GAMES

181 GOALS

MOST APPEARANCES
LARRY LLOYD (9)
Nottingham Forest

TOP SCORER
SØREN LERBY (10)
Ajax

MOST GOALS
AJAX (31)

MOST CLEAN SHEETS
REAL MADRID (5)

16 Semi-finalists Ajax put 16 goals past Helsinki in their first round tie and then scored ten in one game against AC Omonia in the second round. Winners Nottingham Forest only scored 13 goals in total throughout the whole tournament.

1 The number of occasions Nottingham Forest have been crowned champions of England – they are the only side to have won the European Cup more times than their domestic league.

1979-80 European Cup Final | 28 May 1980, Madrid

NOTTINGHAM FOREST 1-0 HAMBURG

J. Robertson 20'

ASTON VILLA 1981-82 AWAY

After becoming one of the major suppliers in the decade before, French kit manufacturers Le Coq Sportif helped introduce a series of design and fabric innovations during the 1980s. The company worked with several successful club and international sides during the era, not least 1982 European Cup winners Aston Villa. Pin stripes and central club crests were common features, and both were included in the white away kit worn by the Lions when they won the final. The strip had a claret trim too – a nod to Villa's classic claret and blue home strips.

ASTON VILLA 1981-82 AWAY

1982 was the sixth consecutive year in which an English club took the European Cup, with Aston Villa winning the competition this time. Football League champions 12 months earlier after using just 14 players, the club overcame the departure of their influential manager Ron Saunders partway through their continental quest to take the trophy.

Saunders had guided Villa back to the big time, winning promotion to Division One in 1975 and two League Cups along the way. After helping secure their first league title in 71 years however, a dispute with the Villa Park hierarchy lead to his resignation – leaving his assistant Tony Barton to pick up the reigns and finish the charge. With their chances of more domestic silverware over, the novice was able to concentrate on the European Cup, their place in the quarter-finals having already been secured under Saunders' watch.

Playing in the competition for the first time, Villa won their first round tie with Icelandic representatives Valur 7-0 on aggregate. Round two was less straightforward, progress over BFC Dynamo coming via away goals, and that was followed by Barton's first European game where an excellent 0-0 draw at Dynamo Kyiv set Villa up for an assured second leg success back in Birmingham. After Trevor Morley's early goal against Anderlecht in the semi-final first leg, another clean sheet in the return was key – Barton had taken his side to the final and they were yet to concede under him in the tournament.

Securing their place on the same night, Bayern Munich's path to the final was goal-laden in comparison. It included a notable 4-0 aggregate victory over Benfica, whilst in the semi-final they saw off CSKA Sofia 7-4 after the Bulgarians had eliminated earlier holders Liverpool. The German giants dominated Europe in the mid-1970s and were tipped to win the top prize once more at De Kuip in the Netherlands.

Their hopes rose further following the early withdrawal of injured Villa goalkeeper Jimmy Rimmer, but understudy Nigel Spink was unfazed by the task and ensured another shut out. Curiously, whilst both Rimmer and Spink wore the same shirts – a green design with black sleeves, Rimmer had black shorts on whilst Spink used the same white version as the outfield players.

There was a late scare when Bayern put the ball in the net before being flagged for offside but by that stage Villa were already ahead, Peter Withe scoring what proved to be the vital goal after Morley's trickery on the wing.

ASTON VILLA 1981-82

11TH PLACE — English Division One
5TH ROUND — English FA Cup
5TH ROUND — English League Cup
WINNERS — European Cup

 RON SAUNDERS (until February 1982), then Tony Barton

PETER WITHE

EUROPEAN CUP IN NUMBERS

61 GAMES

166 GOALS

MOST APPEARANCES
GORDON COWANS (9)
Aston Villa

TOP SCORER
DIETER HOENEB (7)
Bayern Munich

MOST GOALS
BAYERN MUNICH (20)

MOST CLEAN SHEETS
ASTON VILLA (7)

46,000 The recorded attendance for the final was the lowest of the 1980s, and was less than half the gate (97,000) that witnessed Milan beating Steaua Bucharest to win the competition later in the decade.

1 The number of professional games Aston Villa goalkeeper Nigel Spink had played before he came on as an early substitute in the final against Bayern.

1981-82 European Cup Final | 26 May 1982, Rotterdam

ASTON VILLA 1-0 BAYERN MUNICH

P. Withe 67'

HAMBURG 1982-83 HOME

Nottingham Forest must have made an impression on Hamburg when they met in the 1980 European Cup final, as the Germans went on to win the competition three years later whilst wearing an almost identical design from the same company. Using their red change tops against Juventus, the only major addition from adidas were white pinstripes, which were accompanied by Hamburg's minimalistic club crest and initials to complete the slimline look often associated with the decade. Domestic sponsors BP had to be removed to meet competition rules, whilst appropriately enough 'Die Rothosen' completed their strip with shiny red shorts.

PIN STRIPE CHIC

1982-83 is still considered the greatest season in Hamburg's history, when Austrian manager Ernst Happel delivered a successive league title, and won the European Cup just as he had with Feyenoord in 1970.

The Bundesliga championship came after a remarkable unbeaten league record that stretched virtually a whole calendar year and had started midway through the previous campaign – a season in which Hamburg reached the 1982 UEFA Cup final. Beaten over two legs against IFK Gothenburg, the side went onto better things 12 months later.

The team only lost four times in total, holding onto their Bundesliga crown on goal difference over Werder Bremen – the side that had broken the unbeaten run in late January. There was an unexpected defeat at Arminia Bielefeld too, plus a real cup shock where Hamburg lost to an eventually relegated Hertha Berlin, but even the strongest sides have off days and in Europe they proved their class.

The first and second rounds brought progress against BFC Dynamo and then Olympiacos during which a total of eight goals were scored and only one conceded. The quarter-finals provided another surprise as Dynamo Kyiv inflicted Hamburg's only home defeat, but the second leg at the Volksparkstadion had been preceded by a commanding victory in the first game that meant it was immaterial.

The 4-2 aggregate success resulted in a semi-final against Real Sociedad, with Juventus playing Widzew Lodz in the other tie. The Italians had just beaten reigning European Cup holders Aston Villa, whilst Widzew had also eliminated English opposition when they overcame Liverpool. The Poles had been in the goals throughout the tournament but didn't have the fire power to get past Juventus, yet both semis did go down to the wire.

A Michel Platini penalty for Juventus with eight minutes left of the second leg kept a determined Widzew at bay, whilst an even later goal from Thomas von Heesen against Sociedad was enough to see Hamburg through. They had led twice before over the two games, but with 84 minutes gone the midfielder's effort confirmed a 3-2 win.

The final proved just as close. Played in the Olympic Stadium in Athens, where Hamburg had already won in the second round, the only goal came in the opening stages and was good enough to win any game, Felix Magath finding the top corner from distance. This was Hamburg's peak; they have won only one major trophy since, but by becoming the first manager to win the European Cup with different clubs Happel remains a legend.

HAMBURG 1982-83

WINNERS — Bundesliga
ROUND OF 16 — DFB-Pokal
WINNERS — European Cup

👤 **ERNST HAPPEL**
⚽ **HORST HRUBESCH**

EUROPEAN CUP IN NUMBERS

59 GAMES

173 GOALS

MOST APPEARANCES
MASSIMO BONINI (9)
Juventus

TOP SCORER
PAOLO ROSSI/MICHEL PLATINI (5) Juventus

MOST GOALS
WIDZEW LODZ/JUVENTUS (19)

MOST CLEAN SHEETS
HAMBURG (5)

983 The number of people that were in attendance in Reykjavik when Real Sociedad beat Icelandic champions Vikingur 1-0 in their first round first leg tie.

6 The final finished 1-0 for the sixth time in a row, with the sequence being broken the following season when Liverpool beat Roma on penalties following a 1-1 draw after extra time.

1982-83 European Cup Final | 25 May 1983, Athens

HAMBURG 1-0 JUVENTUS

F. Magath 9'

AC MILAN 1988-89 AWAY

Italian sportswear firm Kappa began supplying kit to Milan in 1986 and soon saw them become one of the most respected club sides of all time. In 1989 the team won the European Cup for the first time in 20 years, wearing the lucky strip that has since become part of the 'maglia fortunata' backstory. The side have used white on six of the seven occasions they have become champions of Europe, although the shirts worn in this final were different to their usual design that season – they were without the logo of their locally based sponsors Mediolanum, whilst the collars, cuffs and socks all featured red and black trim to reflect their home colours.

THE WHITE STRIPS

AC MILAN 1988-89 AWAY

Not only did Milan look good in their brilliant white strip, but their football was a joy too. After a run of 11 finals decided by either a single goal or penalty shootout the Italian's cut loose to win the European Cup, making it look easy as they cruised past Steaua Bucharest.

The Romanians were no pushovers, they had won it themselves in 1986 and that was much more recently than Milan had managed, but they had little answer to the masterclass from Arrigo Sacchi's men who had it wrapped up by half time following two goals from Ruud Gullit and one in between from Marco van Basten. The forward got another shortly after the break to confirm his side's return to the top by securing the European trophy. A year later Frank Rijkaard got the winner to ensure they retained the European Cup, further cementing their status as Europe's elite.

Milan's trio of Dutch superstars had arrived earlier in the decade. Playing alongside a host of Italian internationals, they brought great success and, in the same calendar year that they beat Steaua, Sacchi delivered the Intercontinental Cup against Atletico Nacional of Colombia to make them in effect de facto club champions of the world.

The fact Milan have been champions of Europe four times since 1988-89 highlights how tough a wait it had been for their fans since their previous success in 1969. On that occasion the final had been in Madrid, and a return in the first leg of the semi-finals 20 years later was to be a massive test of their hopes. Van Basten scored to help earn a 1-1 draw against Real though, and once back at the San Siro they gave a proper display of their capabilities.

A 5-0 rout of Europe's most successful club made people sit up. Steaua had enjoyed a handsome 5-1 aggregate victory against Galatasaray in their semi-final tie, but 'I Rossoneri' had put the continent well and truly on notice – they were back, and they were about to dominate.

The season before had seen an early UEFA Cup exit to Espanyol, but with the campaign ending with a close run Serie A title they were about to return to the premier competition for the first time in nearly a decade. In 1979-80 they were unable to get past the first round, but now it was a different story – a replay was needed against Red Star after their second round second leg in Belgrade was abandoned due to fog, but by the closing stages of the tournament Milan were a level apart.

AC MILAN 1988-89

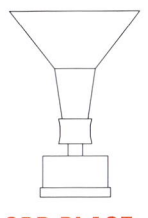

3RD PLACE
Serie A

2ND ROUND
Coppa Italia

WINNERS
European Cup

 ARRIGO SACCHI

 **MARCO VAN BASTEN**

EUROPEAN CUP IN NUMBERS

59 GAMES

170 GOALS

MOST APPEARANCES
MAURO TASSOTTI (9) AC Milan

TOP SCORER
MARCO VAN BASTEN (10) AC Milan

MOST GOALS
STEAUA BUCHAREST (22)

MOST CLEAN SHEETS
AC MILAN (5)

2 Milan wore the same kit for two finals running, retaining the trophy in 1990. The only difference on their shirts was the scudetto being replaced by the European Cup trophy.

0 In the first round AEL Limassol were knocked out by Neuchatel Xamax. After finishing 3-3 over two legs, the tie went to penalties, AEL Limassol failing with all three of their efforts.

1988-89 European Cup Final | 24 May 1989, Barcelona

STEAUA BUCHAREST 0-4 AC MILAN

R. Gullit 18', 39',
M. van Basten 28', 46'

NAPOLI 1990-91 HOME

The Italian national side are not the only team to be known as the 'Azzurri', with Napoli's blue strips having long been established. Worn in homage to Naples' coastal location, the club have worn various shades during their history and in 1990-91 adopted a lighter version of the colour than had seen them win Serie A the season before. Makers Ennerre provided two different home tops during the campaign, one initially described as a 'cup' option when in truth the original ended up being seen across most competitions, plus a mainly white change version and a red third option. All of the tops in the set shared the same polo neck style collar and Napoli's famous Mars sponsorship logo across the chest.

NAPOLI 1990-91 HOME

Napoli warmed up for their 1990-91 defence of the title with a statement 5-1 win over Juventus in the Supercoppa Italiana, but the season soon started to go downhill following an indifferent start in the league and the absence of talisman Diego Maradona.

The Argentine had been instrumental in his club's rise, featuring heavily as they won the UEFA Cup in 1989 and secured domestic success by winning two Serie A titles and the Coppa Italia. Skipper as they thumped Juventus, one of Maradona's subsequent final acts in a Napoli shirt was to help the club get past the first round of the European Cup for the first time in their history.

Beaten by Real Madrid over two legs when they first entered the tournament in 1987-88, this time they went one better after easing past the Hungarian champions Ujpest. 2-0 winners in Budapest in the second leg, a brace for Maradona in the first fixture had set up an equally deserved 3-0 victory and eventual safe passage. Two goalless draws with Spartak Moscow followed however, and after losing 5-3 on penalties the club didn't return to the competition until 2011.

Maradona was a bona fide Napoli legend, and after seeing off European Cup holders Milan to win the 1989-90 Serie A championship, their next push fell well short without him. Already struggling on home soil by the time of their elimination to Moscow, an end of season rally did at least mean a midtable finish, the side rounding off their schedule with a victory over Bologna.

That match was played three days before the European Cup final between Red Star Belgrade and Marseille, which saw the Yugoslav First Federal Football League winners come out on top on penalties. The game had finished 0-0 after extra time, but the Serbians were flawless from the spot to win the shoot-out having already come through an equally difficult looking semi-final just to get there.

Bayern Munich were beaten at that point following a notable first leg win in Germany, with the eventual winners already getting past Dynamo Dresden, Rangers and Grasshoppers to reach that stage. Marseille meanwhile, had been involved in a controversial episode in their quarter-final with holders Milan, who refused to return to the pitch following a floodlight failure in France – the tie was evenly poised and so UEFA awarded the hosts a 3-0 victory that allowed them to meet Napoli's conquerors Spartak in the semis.

NAPOLI 1990-91

8TH PLACE — Serie A
SEMI-FINALS — Coppa Italia
2ND ROUND — European Cup

👤 **ALBERTO BIGON**
⚽ **CARECA**

EUROPEAN CUP IN NUMBERS

59 GAMES
188 GOALS

MOST APPEARANCES
BERNARD CASONI (9)
Marseille

TOP SCORER
PETER PACULT (6)
Swarovski Tirol

MOST GOALS
REAL MADRID (22)

MOST CLEAN SHEETS
SPARTAK MOSCOW (5)

260 An Italian city was selected for the final, so had Napoli progressed in the competition they would have only needed to travel 260 kilometres to the Stadio San Nicola in Bari.

120 In 1991 Red Star Belgrade won the tournament, after enduring a goalless 120 tense minutes against Marseille. The game was settled on penalties, Red Star winning 5-3.

1990-91 European Cup First Round, First Leg | 19 September 1990, Naples

NAPOLI 3-0 UJPESTI

M. Baroni 35'
D. Maradona 44', 77'

SAMPDORIA 1991-92 AWAY

Sampdoria are synonymous with the white, red and black horizontal hoops that run across the middle of their shirts and have one of the most clearly defined looks in football. In 1991-92 their kits followed the same template as one another, including their familiar St. George's Cross emblem. As reigning Italian champions, the blue home version incorporated a scudetto on the left breast with the change option featuring the club crest on the sleeve. Asics tweaked this for the final however, and with both sides using their alternative strips for the game Sampdoria displayed their title winning credentials on a predominately white shirt.

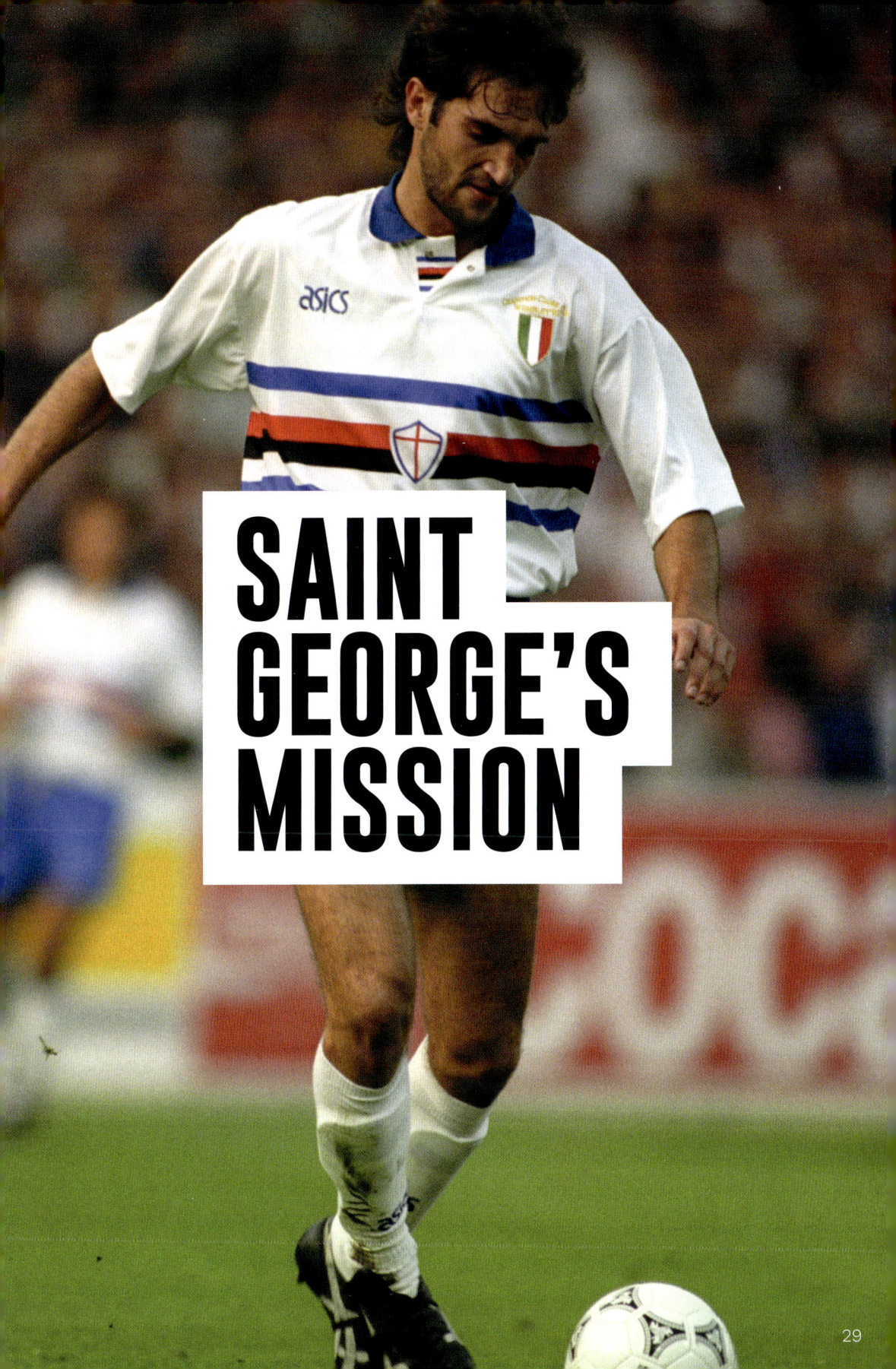

SAINT GEORGE'S MISSION

'I Blucerchiati' have won Serie A once in their history, but they came agonisingly close to following it up with an even bigger prize a year later. The 1992 European Cup final was their third continental final in four years and, having won the Cup Winners' Cup two years earlier, hopes were high of a romantic ending.

Unable to recover from a dreadful league start, Sampdoria were never in with a real chance of retaining their title but fared better in cup football. They reached the semi-finals of the Coppa Italia before a narrow defeat to Parma and successfully negotiated an unfamiliar competition format to make it to Wembley. Whilst there were one or two bumps along the way, their charge was memorable.

Composed displays in rounds one and two against Rosenborg and Honved meant that Sampdoria qualified for the newly introduced stages. Despite topping the Group A mini league, their record was mixed and they were unable to beat bottom side Panathinaikos either home or away. They did, however, twice overcome the reigning European Cup holders Red Star Belgrade, with a stunning 3-1 win in Sofia in their penultimate fixture proving crucial.

There had been a defeat to Anderlecht earlier in the group, whilst over in Group B on the same day Barcelona were winning away at Dynamo Kyiv. The Spaniards enjoyed a slightly more straightforward group stage, and by the time they had suffered their first defeat, they had already secured enough points to finish top. They did though need penalties before that to get past Kaiserslautern in the knockout stages and had lost an away leg at Hansa Rostock.

It was perhaps understandable then that both sides started the final looking nervy, not least Barcelona who were yet to win the competition and had been forced to look on enviously as rivals Real Madrid had dominated across the early years since its inception. They had twice come close, losing two finals, and whilst they too had won the Cup Winners' Cup on three earlier occasions, they'd been beaten in the final of that the season before.

Under that pressure and with their opponents in determined style, Barcelona had to wait until extra time to break the deadlock when Ronald Koeman blasted in. The goal proved vital – Sampdoria's dreams were over, and Barcelona were at last kings of Europe. Slipping into their home strips before being presented with the trophy – they had worn change colours for the game – the next time it would be awarded would be in the Champions League era.

SAMPDORIA 1991-92

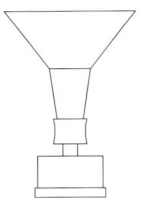

7TH PLACE
Serie A

SEMI-FINALS
Coppa Italia

RUNNERS-UP
European Cup

 VUJADIN BOŠKOV

⚽ **GIANLUCA VIALLI**

EUROPEAN CUP IN NUMBERS

73 GAMES

192 GOALS

MOST APPEARANCES
FAUSTO PARI (11)
Sampdoria

TOP SCORER
SERGEI YURAN (7)
Benfica

MOST GOALS
BENFICA (22)

MOST CLEAN SHEETS
BARCELONA (6)

8 The number of clubs that progressed into the new look group stages to determine who would reach the final. Sides played each other home and away, with the two mini league winners progressing to Wembley.

30 It took European giants Benfica half an hour before they broke the resistance of Maltese minnows Hamrun Spartans in their first round first leg match.

1991-92 European Cup Final | 20 May 1992, London

SAMPDORIA 0-1 BARCELONA

R. Koeman 112'

MARSEILLE 1992-93 HOME

Suppliers adidas continued to lead the way in football kit design during the early 1990s, with several of their efforts since reaching legendary status. The kits used by Marseille plus several others during 1992-93 were instantly recognisable as being theirs thanks to the large branding running across from the right shoulder, the colouring of which matched the other features on an all white shirt, shorts and socks combination. It was a simple yet smart design, unlike the garish outfit goalkeeper Fabien Barthez had to wear as his side won the final, this being a period of increasingly adventurous strips being released.

MARSEILLE 1992-93 HOME

The Champions League was here and, although the final stages were still being referred to as the European Cup, winners Marseille were looking to dominate the rebranded tournament. In the end, however, they were not able to defend their title in 1993-94 – a regrettable end to a period of great success for 'Les Olympiens'.

Ligue 1 winners in the last four years, 1992-93 began with manager Raymond Goethals fronting another title push. It was a close run thing, and the team needed to win their last domestic game of the season against relegation-threatened Valenciennes to ensure another championship, which duly happened. The problem was that the club were later found guilty of attempting to bribe members of the opposition in order to take things easy and were subsequently stripped of the title as a result and refused entry to the following edition of the Champions League.

Before this came to light, however, Marseille went on to complete what was at that point classed as a double, becoming the first French club to win the trophy in the process. They had missed out two years earlier when they'd lost in the final to Red Star Belgrade and the memory of that defeat had driven them on ever since.

Starting with an 8-0 demolition of Glentoran in the first round, Marseille then found the going a little harder against Dinamo Bucharest in round two where they got goals in either half of the second leg from Alen Bokšić to go through. They then faced an awkward group stage including Rangers, Club Brugge and CSKA Moscow, but an unbeaten run that included a vital 1-0 victory in Belgium in the final game saw them come out on top.

An early goal from Bokšić had put them ahead against Brugge after which the side clung on to keep a clean sheet, one of seven they recorded in the competition. It was up front where they excelled, however, scoring more goals than anybody else in the tournament that season en route to the final, against a dominant Milan boasting a 100 per cent record in their group, and with only one goal conceded in any stage of the tournament that season.

Marseille needed to be at their best and they were, breaching that solid defence when Basile Boli rose highest to meet a corner just before half time and then seeing their own back line hold tight from then on. What should have been a season of triumph though, would soon become marred in controversy.

MARSEILLE 1992-93

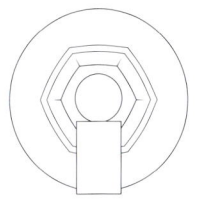
WINNERS
Ligue 1
(later revoked)

QTR-FINALS
Coupe de France

WINNERS
European Cup

RAYMOND GOETHALS

ALEN BOKŠIĆ

EUROPEAN CUP IN NUMBERS

74 GAMES

196 GOALS

MOST APPEARANCES
DIDIER DESCHAMPS/ABEDI PELE (11) Marseille

TOP SCORER
ROMÁRIO (7) PSV

MOST GOALS
MARSEILLE (25)

MOST CLEAN SHEETS
AC MILAN (9)

38 This was the 38th edition of the competition, but the first time with the new Champions League branding.

8 Due to the break-up of the USSR and Yugoslavia, a four tie preliminary round was required to accommodate the new European countries. League winners of Israel and the Faroe Islands entered the tournament at this stage for the first time.

1992-93 European Cup Final | 26 May 1993, Munich

MARSEILLE 1-0 AC MILAN

B. Boli 43'

AJAX 1994-95 AWAY

Ajax became the champions of Europe again for the first time since 1973, but in the meantime kit fashions had changed dramatically. Short shorts and tight tops had been and gone as modest kits made way for busy ensembles with as many features as possible squeezed in; Umbro produced several classic examples of the style for the club in the 1990s, and the dark blue strip worn for the final is one of the best remembered. Including a button collar, side tag, multiple makers logos, centralised club crest and further interpretations of the badge through waves of red print detailing, the tops in particular had a lot going on. This was the first season that sponsors were allowed in European competition too, Umbro providing a further twist by positioning the name of the Abn-Amro bank vertically.

GETTING BUSIER NOW

AJAX 1994-95 AWAY

With work on their new stadium well under way, the 1994-95 season came during a spell of great progress at Ajax. The club had enjoyed a golden period of domestic and international success in the early 1970s and were about to embark on another memorable campaign here, sweeping to another Eredivisie title and returning to the top table in Europe under the enigmatic Louis van Gaal.

Winning the league by seven points and with an extraordinary 106 goals scored, the Amsterdam outfit were almost unplayable in Dutch football. They were mightily impressive in European action too, and ended the campaign with just one defeat, going down to Feyenoord in the KNVB Cup. It was glory all the way other than that, with fans turning up at either the De Meer or Olympisch Stadion being treated to an attractive brand of football their opponents couldn't live with.

They had for a long time split games between the two grounds and had started the season by winning the Dutch Supercup at the Olympisch Stadion, beating Feyenoord 3-0. They also managed a commanding league double over their Rotterdam rivals that more than made up for the KNVB Cup loss, the second game of which was their penultimate league fixture ahead of a Champions League final that had been confirmed a month earlier.

Ajax won all five of their domestic matches between the semi-finals and final, with a 5-0 victory at Feyenoord helping achieve an ominous total of 17 goals scored to only three conceded. It was not as if they needed a confidence boost either, as their path to the Vienna showdown against holders Milan had at times felt like a precession, starting ironically enough with a 2-0 win over the Italians in the group stages.

More changes to the tournament structure meant that the group phase came immediately after the qualifying round. Ajax were given a bye into Group D and made light work of it, unlike Milan who only went through on goal difference over surprise package Casino Salzburg. The Austrians drew both their games with Ajax, who won all four other matches to progress.

Goalless draws in the opening legs of the quarters and semis at Hajduk Split and Bayern Munich were the platform for two outstanding returns in the Netherlands, 3-0 and 5-2 respective victories meaning a rematch with a now improving Milan. They were making their third consecutive appearance in the final, but with young starlet Patrick Kluivert coming off the bench to score a late winner it was Ajax that took the plaudits.

AJAX 1994-95

WINNERS
Eredivisie

QTR-FINALS
KNVB Cup

WINNERS
UEFA Champions League

👤 **LOUIS VAN GAAL**
⚽ **JARI LITMANEN**
⚽⚽⚽⚽⚽⚽⚽⚽⚽⚽
⚽⚽⚽⚽⚽⚽⚽⚽⚽⚽
⚽⚽⚽

EUROPEAN CUP IN NUMBERS

61 GAMES

140 GOALS

MOST APPEARANCES
PAOLO MALDINI (11)
AC Milan

TOP SCORER
GEORGE WEAH (7)
Paris Saint-Germain

MOST GOALS
AJAX (18)

MOST CLEAN SHEETS
AJAX (8)

0 The introduction of group stages had meant teams could lose games and still progress, but Ajax displayed total control regardless. They were unbeaten throughout their campaign.

38,000 Crowds soared as interest in the new look competition continued to rise, with average attendances per match standing at over 38,000 and a total of more than 2.3 million people watching the 61 games (not including qualifying fixtures).

1994-95 UEFA Champions League Final | 24 May 1995, Vienna

AJAX 1-0 AC MILAN

P. Kluivert 85'

JUVENTUS 1995-96 AWAY

The Old Lady had a modern look for the 1996 Champions League final. Their royal blue change kit was typical of the era – loose fitting, and much bolder than strips used to be. The two large yellow stars on the shoulders were more than just decoration though, with each one representing a set of ten league titles and their dominance in Italy. Kappa had introduced the design a season earlier but by now there were some differences – Danone had been replaced by Sony and the highly decorated shirts proudly displayed both the league and cup winners' shields following their 1994-95 domestic double. For this final, UEFA decreed that the names on the back were displayed within a white panel, heat pressed black lettering meaning Juventus' famous colours were still seen in the game.

OLD MEETS NEW

JUVENTUS 1995-96 AWAY

An Italian double in 1995 including a first scudetto in nearly a decade meant Juventus were on a roll. They had reached the UEFA Cup as well and were now ready to go all the way in Europe the following season, beginning their Group C schedule with a 3-1 success over Borussia Dortmund that quickly asserted their intentions.

Fabrizio Ravanelli would prove to be Juventus' top scorer across all competitions, but the contribution of his strike partner Alessandro Del Piero was vital. He scored in all but one of their group ties to give them top spot, four points ahead of the Germans, and even though they trailed 1-0 after the first leg of their quarter-final against Real Madrid, the iconic forward soon had them level once back in Turin. Michele Padovano then nudged his side ahead early in the second half and, with both sides later being reduced to ten men, the Stadio Delle Alpi enjoyed one of its most celebrated nights.

Next up were unfancied Nantes, who put up a strong fight before being edged out 4-3 on aggregate to see Juventus into the final – all roads indeed leading to Rome. There they met Ajax, and for the second time in a row the reigning champions were defeated, Ravanelli's opportunistic early opener being cancelled out before the game went to penalties. The equaliser had come following a fumble from Angelo Peruzzi, but he more than redeemed himself with two spot kick stops that allowed substitute Vladimir Jugović to hit the winner.

With 'home' team Ajax wearing their usual colours, the 'keeper had a yellow and blue reversal of the change tops used by his outfield teammates. His stops helped Juventus earn a dramatic second competition trophy, the side having won it in their more familiar black and white stripes back in 1985. Since then, however, they have earned a tag of nearly men, having lost more finals than any other club.

They had to settle with being runners-up in Italy in 1996 too, rallying after Christmas to reach second place but still ending up eight points shy of champions Milan. This was an era of Italian strength, and with Serie A regularly being touted as being the best league in the world at this point, Juventus went on to make the next two Champions League finals – Milan having reached the three before that after Sampdoria had started the run.

JUVENTUS 1995-96

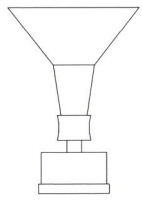  

RUNNERS-UP — Serie A
ROUND OF 16 — Coppa Italia
WINNERS — UEFA Champions League

 MARCELLO LIPPI

 FABRIZIO RAVANELLI
⚽⚽⚽⚽⚽⚽⚽⚽⚽⚽
⚽⚽⚽⚽⚽

EUROPEAN CUP IN NUMBERS

61 GAMES

159 GOALS

MOST APPEARANCES
EDGAR DAVIDS (11)
Ajax

TOP SCORER
JARI LITMANEN (9)
Ajax

MOST GOALS
AJAX/JUVENTUS (22)

MOST CLEAN SHEETS
AJAX (8)

3 There were more changes to the tournament format, with three points being awarded in the group stage from this season onwards. Victories had previously only been worth two points each.

1973 The final was a repeat of the 1973 edition when the two clubs had met in Belgrade. Things panned out very differently on that occasion – it was Ajax that had to wear their change strip of all red and it was the Dutch club that won the trophy, courtesy of an early goal from Johnny Rep.

1995-96 UEFA Champions League Final | 22 May 1996, Rome

AJAX 1-1 JUVENTUS

J. Litmanen 41' **(2-4 PENS)** F. Ravanelli 13'

BORUSSIA DORTMUND 1996-97 HOME

Juventus wore a similar strip in the final as the one they had used 12 months before, but it was Borussia Dortmund's luminous yellow that really caught the eye. Having first entered the European market in 1983, Nike were now big players on the kit scene and they made Dortmund shine, producing two separate sets of strips for domestic and European games – both of which were extremely bright. The outfits worn for the final, however, were actually new and were to be used the following season: they were much cleaner than the previous design although the sponsor used against Juventus, insurers Die Continentale, was subsequently replaced. Player names had been allowed on the back of shirts but were not mandatory, so Dortmund used squad numbers only for the time being.

NIKE'S DESIGN HIGHLIGHT

BORUSSIA DORTMUND 1996-97 HOME

As if being crowned the best in Europe wasn't enough for Borussia Dortmund, the cherry on the cake was the fact they did so at the then-home of their great rivals Bayern Munich, whom had just retaken their Bundesliga title.

The two seasons before had seen Ottmar Hitzfeld's team win their first championships in over 30 years, doing so by a point in 1995 and six in 1996. With their efforts now being focused on the Champions League though, BVB slid out of the race for the top spot and were overtaken by Bayern only to then steal their thunder by winning Europe's top competition instead. In 1964 they had reached the European Cup semi-finals and then two years later secured the Cup Winners' Cup, but now they would achieve the main prize.

A shock cup loss to regional side Wattenscheid 09 early in the season proved just how much Dortmund were wanting to concentrate on matters further afield. Exactly a month later they began Group B with a win over Widzew Lodz, their only defeat of that stage being at home to Atletico Madrid. The two clubs dominated, finishing level on points with four wins and a draw each but the Spaniards coming out on top by virtue of a better goal difference.

This meant a quarter-final tie with Group A winners Auxerre in which Dortmund won both legs. Things then ramped up with a difficult draw to Manchester United, but victories in both matches followed and that meant they were off to Munich. Both ties had seen Dortmund play the first legs at home, but away goals from Lars Ricken helped make the difference – and now they were on the road again, albeit remaining in slightly more familiar surroundings.

Juventus, meanwhile, had bludgeoned their way to the final in their quest to retain the Champions League. Winners of Group C by a distance, they had more than enough to see off Rosenborg before taking apart Ajax in their semi-final. The two finalists had previous encounters – they'd been in the same Champions League group the season before and in 1993 contested the UEFA Cup final.

Over the two legs of their semi-final Juventus had been the clear favourite, but it was BVB's turn to claim the biggest prize in European football. Having already played at the Olympiastadion and earned a point off Bayern earlier in the campaign, Dortmund took control through a clinical Karl-Heinz Riedle brace. Alessandro Del Piero's flick then gave his side hope but, seconds after coming on, Ricken confirmed his side's superiority with a wonderful chip finish.

BORUSSIA DORTMUND 1996-97

3RD PLACE Bundesliga
1ST ROUND DFB-Pokal
WINNERS UEFA Champions League

👤 **OTTMAR HITZFELD**
⚽ **STÉPHANE CHAPUISAT**
⚽⚽⚽⚽⚽⚽⚽⚽⚽⚽⚽⚽⚽⚽⚽

EUROPEAN CUP IN NUMBERS

61 GAMES

161 GOALS

MOST APPEARANCES
CIRO FERRARA (11)
Juventus

TOP SCORER
MILINKO PANTIĆ (5)
Atletico Madrid

MOST GOALS
B. DORTMUND (23)

MOST CLEAN SHEETS
JUVENTUS (6)

6 Juventus' return to the final meant this was the sixth time in a row that Italy were represented in the final. The run continued up to seven in 1998.

0 Following changes made in the wake of the Bosman ruling in 1995, limits on the number of foreign players a club was allowed to field in Europe were removed in their entirety. 1996-97 was the first time Champions League sides had zero restrictions in that regard, having previously worked under a three player (plus two assimilated) maximum rule.

1996-97 UEFA Champions League Final | 28 May 1997, Munich

B. DORTMUND 3-1 JUVENTUS

K.H. Riedle 29', 34'
L. Ricken 70'

A. Del Piero 65'

MANCHESTER UNITED 1998-99 HOME

The combination of Manchester United, Umbro and their sponsors Sharp seemed to go hand in hand during the 1990s, a time in which the club enjoyed a remarkable period of success. The pinnacle of this was surely their dramatic Champions League win in 1999, the chase of which saw the Red Devils continue to use a special 'European' home strip that had been introduced in 1997. The shirt was a rich red which if you looked at closely incorporated several micro detailing depictions of the competition's logo, and it included a grand shield behind the club badge. Goalkeeper Peter Schmeichel's top, meanwhile, included the retro braiding and zipped collar used by Umbro on their domestic design.

DEVILS IN DETAIL

MANCHESTER UNITED 1998-99 HOME

Manchester United had to do it the hard way. Battling on several fronts as they aimed for a treble, they only managed five Champions League victories, but it was still enough to see them take glory.

The crucial factor to Alex Ferguson's achievement was just how hard it was to defeat his side, who didn't always win but made sure they rarely lost either. Crucially, from Christmas onwards United were unbeaten, and whilst draws often meant additional replays or tense European ties the side were always able to dig in and get over the line.

All that hard work paid off during a glorious ten day period in May, starting with a win over Tottenham Hotspur on the final day of the league season to win the Premier League by just a point. Newcastle United were then beaten in the FA Cup final six days later and with two trophies now in hand the Red Devils were able to home in on Bayern Munich for the ultimate showdown in the Champions League final.

Both finalists were looking to complete a historic treble, although after the heartbreaking fashion in which they suffered defeat in Spain, the newly crowned Bundesliga champions Bayern would also go on to lose their domestic cup final. There was no such despair for relentless United, however, who had been forced to show their mettle in Europe right from the start.

After overcoming a potential qualifying round banana skin against LKS Lodz, they were placed in a 'group of death' alongside Bayern, Barcelona and Brondby. Two victories over the Danes and draws in the other matches put them through, only to face more heavy weights as the tournament went on. A tense tie with Inter Milan turned in the final stages of the second leg, with Paul Scholes scoring in Italy to make the aggregate score 3-1, and in the semi-finals, they were back in the country to face Juventus.

A 1-1 first leg draw at Old Trafford had things on a knife edge, but with Roy Keane driving the side on even after picking up a yellow card that meant he would miss the final, they secured a momentous victory. Keane's performance that night has gone down in United folklore, as of course has the most dramatic of finals, which true to form was no easy thing. The side trailed for a long time to a Mario Basler free kick and saw Bayern twice hit the woodwork, but with the clock running down and the pressure building Teddy Sheringham and Ole Gunnar Solskjær pounced.

MANCHESTER UNITED 1998-99

WINNERS
Premier League

WINNERS
English FA Cup

QTR-FINALS
English League Cup

WINNERS
UEFA Champions League

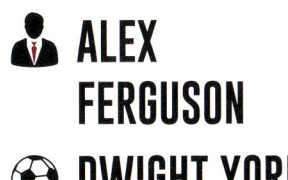
👤 **ALEX FERGUSON**
⚽ **DWIGHT YORKE**

EUROPEAN CUP IN NUMBERS

85 GAMES

238 GOALS

MOST APPEARANCES
PETER SCHMEICHEL (11)
Manchester United

TOP SCORER
DWIGHT YORKE / ANDRIY SHEVCHENKO (8) Manchester United & Dynamo Kyiv

MOST GOALS
MAN UNITED (29)

MOST CLEAN SHEETS
BAYERN MUNICH (5)

8 Following the expansion of the tournament in 1997-98, eight runners-up from UEFA's strongest ranking coefficient leagues were again entered into the competition.

216 The number of goals scored before the competition proper started, now that qualifying took place over two rounds and included champions of lower coefficient nations having also been brought back.

1998-99 UEFA Champions League Final | 26 May 1999, Barcelona

MAN UNITED 2-1 BAYERN MUNICH

T. Sheringham 90 + 1'
O.G. Solskjær 90 + 3'

M. Basler 6'

VALENCIA 2000-01 HOME

The bold thinking behind kits had started to settle down towards the start of the new millennium, with strips beginning to feel more refined again. Champions League finalists Valencia did experiment with some more jazzy change options during the seasons either side, but Nike kept the flourishes down to a minimum on their home strips, the version worn against Bayern Munich being understated yet neat, with a polo collar and black trim that matched the shorts. It was in stark contrast to the loud orange gear worn when they'd reached the final 12 months before, although popular Spanish theme park Terra Mitica remained as sponsor.

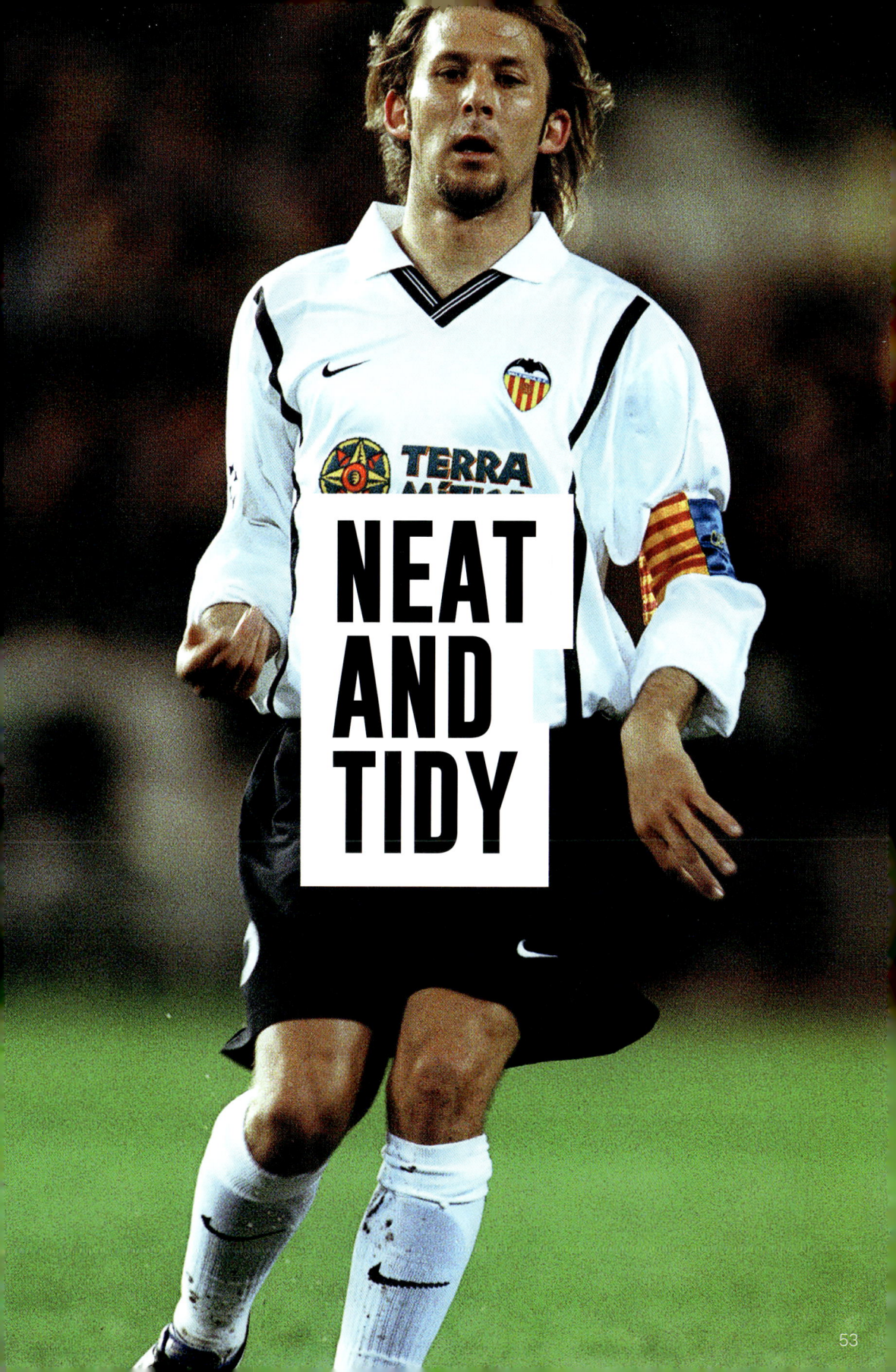

VALENCIA 2000-01 HOME

Valencia were the new boys on the Champions League block at the turn of the century, reaching the final of the competition two seasons in a row as they looked to establish themselves amongst the elite.

Winners of the Cup Winners' Cup in 1980, their only previous experience of Europe's premier competition had been in 1971-72 when they reached the second round of the European Cup, but a series of strong La Liga finishes had earned them a shot at the Champions League and they were keen to make the most of it. Comfortably beaten by compatriots Real Madrid in 2000, Héctor Cúper guided his team to the final once more a year later, although a poor run in January 2001 had already decimated their domestic hopes by that point.

After beginning with another defeat to Real on the opening day of the league Valencia started building up steam. They had eased past Tirol Innsbruck in the qualifying round of the Champions League by this stage and continued to perform in Europe too, topping Group C in the first group stage, but the new year saw a shock Copa del Rey exit on penalties to Guadix and when a run of three consecutive league defeats followed they lost ground.

Continental hopes grew when they finished the second group stage strongly. An additional group phase had been introduced the season before and Valencia had taken to it quickly, going unbeaten as they topped Group A this time to set up a quarter-final with Arsenal. Behind after the first leg in London, an atmospheric night at the Mestalla Stadium saw John Carew score with 15 minutes left to confirm progress on away goals. The semis then followed a similar path – Valencia travelling back to England before overcoming Leeds United in the return following a 3-0 win on another memorable evening.

The final had been an all Spanish affair in 2000 and a rematch appeared close until Bayern Munich knocked out holders Real in the other semi-final. They were never behind in that tie yet at the San Siro trailed to an early goal when Gaizka Mendieta converted from the spot – this became a running theme and after Stefan Effenberg levelled with a penalty, the competition was decided via a shoot-out.

Valencia had undertaken a massive shift to get that far, but after 17 matches they fell at the very last hurdle - Mauricio Pellegrino seeing his attempt blocked by Man of the Match Oliver Kahn as Bayern took glory.

VALENCIA 2000-01

5TH PLACE
La Liga

2ND ROUND
Copa del Rey

RUNNERS-UP
UEFA Champions League

👤 **HÉCTOR CÚPER**
⚽ **JUAN SÁNCHEZ**

EUROPEAN CUP IN NUMBERS

157 GAMES

MOST APPEARANCES
JOHN CAREW (17)
Valencia

TOP SCORER
RAÚL (7)
Real Madrid

449 GOALS

MOST GOALS
REAL MADRID (35)

MOST CLEAN SHEETS
VALENCIA (9)

2 Before winning the tournament for themselves, Bayern Munich had to eliminate the two preceding Champions League winners in the knockout stages. Both holders Real Madrid and Manchester United were beaten 3-1 on aggregate.

315 With the first qualifying phase commencing on 12 July 2000, this was how many days it took until the 2000-01 Champions League winners were decided.

2000-01 UEFA Champions League Final | 23 May 2001, Milan

BAYERN MUNICH 1-1 VALENCIA
S. Effenberg 50' (pen) **(5-4 PENS)** G. Mendieta 3' (pen)

REAL MADRID 2001-02 HOME

With Real Madrid celebrating their centenary in 2002, suppliers adidas released a string of kits during the season. There were standard home, change and third kits, plus three more vintage style 'anniversary' efforts, with a separate European home one thrown in too for good measure. Worn in the final, the latter was a halfway house between the modern design worn most weeks and the reimagined take on the club's original plain white shirts, including only a retro collar and iconic three stripe branding as way of features. Fans loved the subtle elegance of it, but collectors had a problem on their hands - buying all the different tops could prove costly, and to make matters worse the standard kits had to be modified midway through the season when the club replaced the sponsors logo of home appliance company Teka with that of their own website.

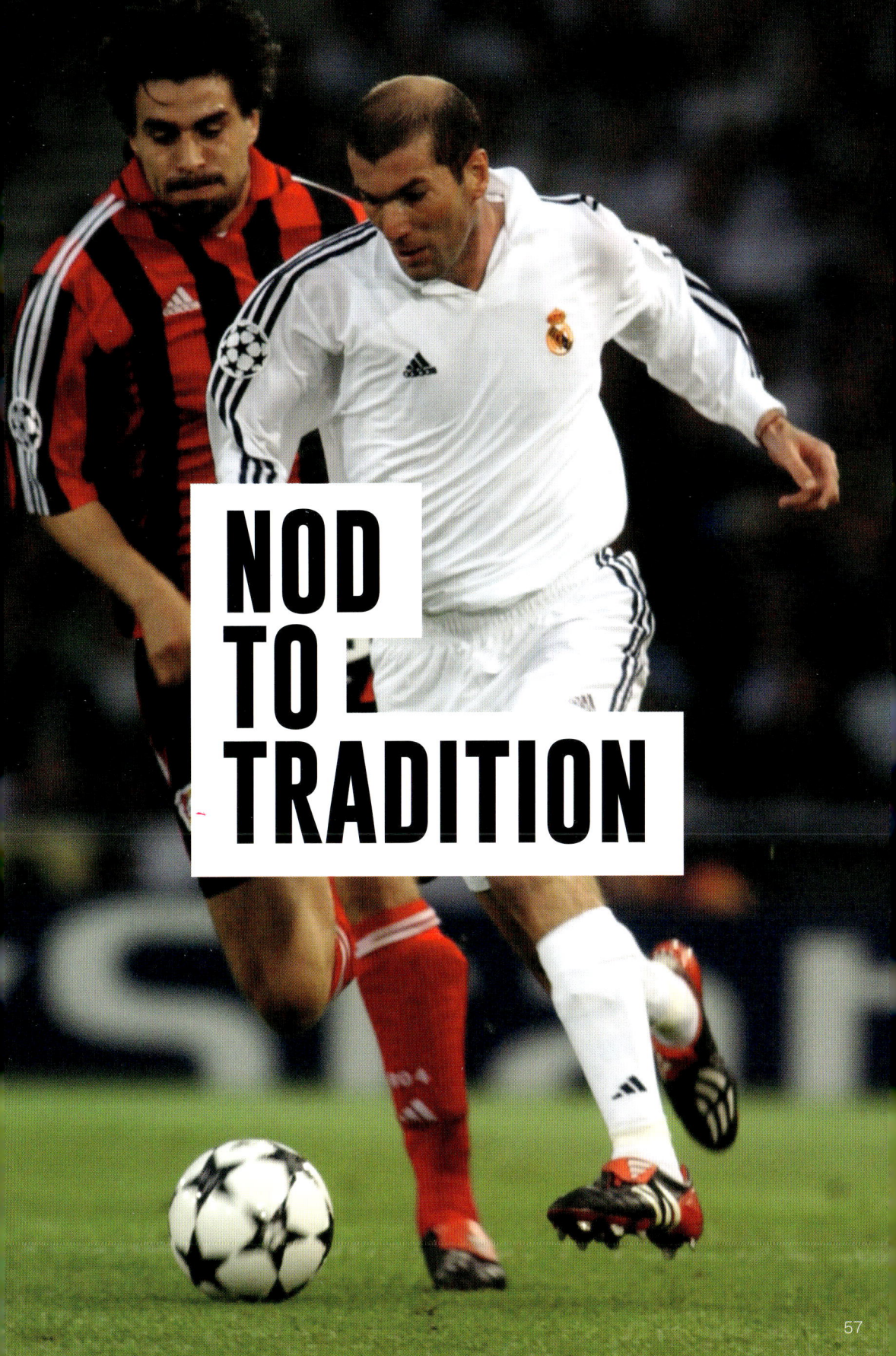

REAL MADRID 2001-02 HOME

Real Madrid are the most successful side in the competition by far, and so it was fitting that they took the Champions League honours as they marked their centenary year. 2002 was their ninth success and victory in the final came courtesy of a wonder goal – Zinedine Zidane's volley as half time approached still being remembered as an all-time classic.

The winner was a reminder of how often Real had lit up the competition over the years, whilst on the day it was the highlight of an otherwise tense fixture. The final was held in Scotland and saw Bayer Leverkusen competing in it for the first time, but after the Germans had fallen behind for a second time they struggled to respond – Lúcio had quickly levelled following Raúl's opener, but once back in front Real's experience told.

In the following decade the side would enjoy another era of European dominance, winning the Champions League four times in five seasons. 2002 had been the second time in three years that they had won the competition as well, and whilst they'd won their domestic title in between those two successes, home form did suffer either side.

2001-02 witnessed several sticky patches as Real fell well behind champions Valencia and lost the Copa del Rey final to Deportivo De La Coruna. Being beaten a total of 14 times in Spanish football was considered poor, but they at least managed to overcome the two defeats suffered abroad – going down at Lokomotiv Moscow having already won Group A in the first group stage and coming from behind after the quarter-final first leg to get past reigning champions Bayern Munich.

Group C of the second group stage had been more convincing – five wins out of six being secured – and after Guti's dramatic late winner against Bayern the side stepped it up a gear. There were nearly 100,000 spectators present in Barcelona for the semi-final first leg between two great rivals and when Steve McManaman added to Zidane's earlier goal in additional time Real had one foot in the final. The job was completed with a 1-1 second leg draw, and they were now set to go in the decider for a 12th time.

Leverkusen, meanwhile, had enjoyed a remarkable route to the match. After coming through the third qualifying round and enjoying famous wins over Barcelona and Juventus in the group stages they eliminated both Liverpool and Manchester United, but the stirring underdog story came to an end as Real ruled yet again.

REAL MADRID 2001-02

3RD PLACE
La Liga

RUNNERS-UP
Copa del Rey

WINNERS
UEFA Champions League

 **VICENTE DEL BOSQUE**

 RAÚL

EUROPEAN CUP IN NUMBERS

157 GAMES

393 GOALS

MOST APPEARANCES
YILDIRAY BAŞTÜRK (17)
Bayer Leverkusen

TOP SCORER
RUUD VAN NISTELROOY (10) Manchester United

MOST GOALS
REAL MADRID (35)

MOST CLEAN SHEETS
LIVERPOOL (8)

56 With defensive tactics taking over, there were 56 fewer goals scored in the 2001-02 competition than had been scored in the tournament the season before.

5 Four players were all accredited with making five assists during the competition, with Bayern Munich's Hasan Salihamidžić coming top of the charts by virtue of playing the least minutes.

2001-02 UEFA Champions League Final | 15 May 2002, Glasgow

B. LEVERKUSEN 1-2 REAL MADRID

Lúcio 14'

Raúl 8'
Z. Zidane 45'

ROMA 2002-03 HOME

With baggy fit tops being phased out, Kappa's tight fit style quickly became very recognisable. Roma were one of several sides across the continent they were working with at this point, introducing a batch of traditional domestic strips alongside European versions that were a little more contemporary. The tops all came from a template that included the same piping and side panelling arrangements with raglan sleeves and Mazda branding, but the accentuating black collar and contrasting sleeves on the Champions League edit gave a bolder look. Roma were unable to get out of the second group stage of the competition, but their deep red and golden yellow kits – worn to reflect the colours of Rome – were still a hit.

ROMA 2002-03 HOME

Rivals Milan and Juventus contested the Champions League final in 2002-03 in a competition dominated by Italian clubs that saw neighbours Inter also reach the final four. The familiarity of Serie A's top three that season perhaps contributed to tight outcomes too, with the Milan semi-final derby being decided on away goals and the final itself going to penalties.

The idea of away goals seems ironic given that Milan and Inter ground share, but it was the former that progressed to play Juventus after they had ended holders Real Madrid's defence of the trophy. Milan had finished 11 points shy of Juventus at home but had the edge in Manchester, forcing a goalless draw after extra time before winning a shoot-out in which goalkeepers Dida and Gianluigi Buffon both caused controversy by being off their line when making a total of five saves. Andriy Shevchenko then hit the decisive kick as his side won the competition for a sixth time.

For their part, Fabio Capello's Roma managed to get to the second group stage having been runners-up in Serie A the season before. They were then runners-up in Group C of the first group stage too, finishing behind Real on goal difference. The two sides had traded wins, Roma earning a superb victory in Spain thanks to a goal from club legend Francesco Totti, and that was followed up with a hard fought draw against AEK Athens where defeat would have meant elimination.

Roma struggled at home in Europe but looked good on the road. They'd beaten Genk in a feisty match punctuated by seven yellow cards and a sending off in that first section, and in Group B of the second group produced an eye catching 3-0 win in Valencia during which Totti grabbed a brace. That had come after three defeats though, and whilst the final game day of the group started with all four able to go through Roma finished bottom.

The side had reached the same stage the season before and have been in regular Champions League action since, whilst in 2021-22 they became the first winners of the UEFA Europa Conference League after beating Feyenoord in the final. In 2002-03 they qualified for it's equivalent, the UEFA Cup, after reaching the final of the Coppa Italia, losing to Milan who made it an impressive double. League form for Roma, however, was inconsistent, and in games against their fellow Champions League entrants they only collected four points.

ROMA 2002-03

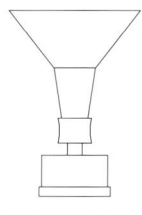  

8TH PLACE
Serie A

RUNNERS-UP
Coppa Italia

2ND GROUP STAGE
UEFA Champions League

 **FABIO CAPELLO**
 **FRANCESCO TOTTI**

EUROPEAN CUP IN NUMBERS

157 GAMES

431 GOALS

MOST APPEARANCES
PAOLO MALDINI (17)
AC Milan

TOP SCORER
RUUD VAN NISTELROOY (12) Manchester United

MOST GOALS
REAL MADRID (33)

MOST CLEAN SHEETS
AC MILAN (8)

14 Top competition scorer for the second season running with 12 goals in the main section, Ruud van Nistelrooy's total haul included two more strikes in the third qualifying round.

3 Of Italy's four representatives in the competition, Roma were the only ones not to reach the semi-finals. The other three teams, AC Milan, Inter Milan and Juventus all enjoyed impressive wins in the quarters, with AC Milan going on to win the whole thing.

2002-03 UEFA Champions League First Group Stage: Group C | 30 October 2002, Madrid

REAL MADRID 0-1 ROMA

F. Totti 27'

PORTO 2003-04 HOME

Innovative Dri-FIT technology had started being introduced by Nike, meaning that this Porto strip had a smoother fabric than many previous kits. The company produced a range of similar shirts for all their Champions League sides with disappearing neck lines and scooped mesh sections on the lower half, as well as broad stripes with additional detailing being implemented for the Portuguese champions. As per UEFA guidelines, player issue shirts in the competition needed back panels to make the numbers clearer and whilst these also bore the insignia of long term backers and ceramics makers Revigrés, domestic and replica versions instead displayed the markings of a local telecoms operation. There was a further deviation come the final, with the famous Nike Swoosh going from red (which matched the names and numbering) to white.

EUROPE'S SMOOTH OPERATORS

PORTO 2003-04 HOME

Winners of the European Cup in 1987, Porto won the trophy for a second time whilst also taking their domestic league title at a canter. Their Primeira Liga defence was a procession, and the club were close to more silverware having narrowly lost the Taça de Portugal final to Benfica and the UEFA Super Cup to Milan.

That Super Cup spot had come by virtue of winning the 2003 UEFA Cup final and coach José Mourinho confidently predicted that his side could now compete on the main stage – he was soon proven right, and the Portuguese giants became the first club from outside Europe's top four leagues to win the tournament since 1995.

The final was against Monaco, whose ground had staged Porto's Super Cup match, yet neither team had been tipped to do so well. The competition reverted to a single group format for 2003-04 with both clubs bypassing the qualifying rounds and ensuring safe passage into the knockout phases, Porto winning their round of 16 tie with Manchester United following a memorable night at Old Trafford and Monaco getting past Lokomotiv Moscow on away goals.

Monaco had finished behind Lyon by a point in Ligue 1 the season before but in Europe they were now about to surpass them. Porto beat Lyon 4-2 on aggregate in the next round whereas Monaco completed a sensational 5-5 aggregate against Real Madrid that again saw them go through via away goals. They then beat Chelsea 5-3 over two legs to win their semi-final, whereas Porto had to be considerably tighter.

After a 0-0 draw with Deportivo La Coruna in the first leg in Portugal the second game played out like a chess match. Brazilian forward Derlei proved to be the winner, finding the corner with a confident penalty kick to nudge his side ahead prior to a tense final 30 minutes. His teammates saw it out to book their final spot, and at Schalke's Veltins-Arena they swept Monaco away with goals from Carlos Alberto and Dimitri Alenichev, as well as one from Man of the Match Deco.

The game was eight days after Porto's domestic cup final and 18 after they had rounded off their league schedule. Benfica may have won the cup but had been a distant second in the title race, and now they had seen their great rivals draw level in terms of being crowned champions of Europe.

PORTO 2003-04

WINNERS
Primeira Liga

RUNNERS-UP
Taça de Portugal

WINNERS
UEFA Champions League

JOSÉ MOURINHO
BENNI McCARTHY

EUROPEAN CUP IN NUMBERS

125 GAMES

309 GOALS

MOST APPEARANCES
PATRICE EVRA (13)
Manchester United

TOP SCORER
FERNANDO MORIENTES (9)
Monaco

MOST GOALS
MONACO (27)

MOST CLEAN SHEETS
DEPORTIVO DE LA CORUNA (7)

16 The second group stage was replaced with a knockout round of 16, the slimmed down arrangement reducing the number of games played in the tournament by 32.

32,000 The Principality of Monaco had a population at the time of around 32,000, which was approximately 20,000 less than the capacity of Porto's home ground at the same time.

2003-04 UEFA Champions League Final | 26 May 2004, Gelsenkirchen

MONACO 0-3 PORTO

C. Alberto 39'
Deco 71'
Alenichev 75'

Lineup:
- V. Baía
- R. Carvalho
- N. Valente
- J. Costa
- Costinha
- Maniche
- Deco
- Derlei
- P. Mendes
- C. Alberto
- P. Ferreira

LIVERPOOL 2004-05 GOALKEEPER

Not only was this a classic final, but there were two classic kits on show too, with Liverpool in their traditional all red and AC Milan wearing their usually lucky white. The night belonged to Liverpool goalkeeper Jerzy Dudek though, meaning it was his own jersey that featured in some of the most iconic moments of the night. Made by Reebok, who had enjoyed a nearly decade-long connection with the club at this point, the black top with burgundy sleeves was classed as their alternative option – the same design but in a green and black colourway being deemed the home choice. The kit also had white piping and micro patterning, as well as having match details embroidered on for the final.

KEEPING IT CLASSY

The Reds have a fine pedigree in the tournament, but even by their standards the 50th iteration of Europe's premier competition saw them pull something special off. Three goals behind and with all hope seemingly gone at half time, the side rallied to complete the comeback of all comebacks and produce a performance still regarded as one of the greatest football finals ever played.

Paolo Maldini's opener seconds into the match and a double from Hernán Crespo had put Milan in total control, but a half time reshuffle and Steven Gerrard's rallying header started the memorable fightback, as six minutes later his side were back on level terms – Vladimír Šmicer scoring from range and Xabi Alonso reacting quickly after his penalty had initially been saved to slot it in for Liverpool.

Captain Gerrard had won the spot kick and continued to drive his side on. Both teams had chances to then grab a winner, but Milan seemed shell shocked and despite winning the competition via penalties two seasons before they now struggled from the spot, with goalkeeper Jerzy Dudek proving the difference. Recreating the 'spaghetti legs' of Bruce Grobbelaar when Liverpool beat Roma in the 1984 final and Alan Kennedy scored the shoot-out winner, Dudek made two stops including the clincher from Andriy Shevchenko.

Milan had been at their defensive best en route to the final with a tournament high of nine clean sheets, but they were facing a side who under Rafael Benítez had a 'never say die' attitude and were capable of moments of absolute quality. They only just got past Grazer AK in Champions League qualifying and lost twice in Group A too, but after winning their final game of that stage against Olympiacos to get through, Liverpool started to grow into their game.

Gerrard was influential throughout – his late stunner against the Greeks was vital and after Bayer Leverkusen were seen off comfortably, he was pivotal in the first leg as Liverpool beat Juventus in the quarter-finals. After that had been navigated the side faced Chelsea in the semis for an anxious encounter settled by a hotly disputed Luis García goal and that was it, the club was back in the final for the first time since 1985.

It looked for a while as if it would be one to forget for Liverpool fans, only for them to witness an improbable turn around. Sponsors Carlsberg had adorned their kit since 1992 and were famous for their marketing tag line suggestion that it was 'probably the best lager in the world', with supporters witnessing that final probably saying that football is the best game in the world.

LIVERPOOL 2004-05

5TH PLACE
Premier League

3RD ROUND
English FA Cup

RUNNERS-UP
English League Cup

WINNERS
UEFA Champions League

 RAFAEL BENÍTEZ

 MILAN BAROŠ
LUIS GARCÍA
STEVEN GERRARD

EUROPEAN CUP IN NUMBERS

125 GAMES

331 GOALS

MOST APPEARANCES
KAKÁ (13)
AC Milan

TOP SCORER
RUUD VAN NISTELROOY (8)
Manchester United

MOST GOALS
LYON (29)

MOST CLEAN SHEETS
AC MILAN (9)

53 AC Milan kept the most clean sheets in the competition, thanks in part to goalkeeper Dida, who made a total of more than 50 saves during the tournament.

1926 Six goals were scored in a breathless final, which was the most seen since Benfica had beaten Real Madrid 5-3 forty-three years before.

2004-05 UEFA Champions League Final | 25 May 2005, Istanbul

AC MILAN 3-3 LIVERPOOL
(2-3 PENS)

P. Maldini 1'
H. Crespo 39', 44'

S. Gerrard 54', V. Šmicer 56'
X. Alonso 61'

BARCELONA 2005-06 AWAY

Having used a change strip when they first won the trophy in 1992, Barcelona proudly wore their historic blue and garnet red stripes this time out in the final – although their Nike change kit for the 2005-06 campaign was a particular highlight of kit design at the time. The v-neck fluorescent yellow shirts with black trim and black shorts did, however, still include a nod to the home colours, with them featuring on the sleeve inserts. Fiercely proud of their roots, Barcelona's kits were still sponsorless at this stage due to their stance on advertising, whilst on the inside collars the yellow and red hues of the Catalonian flag were also incorporated.

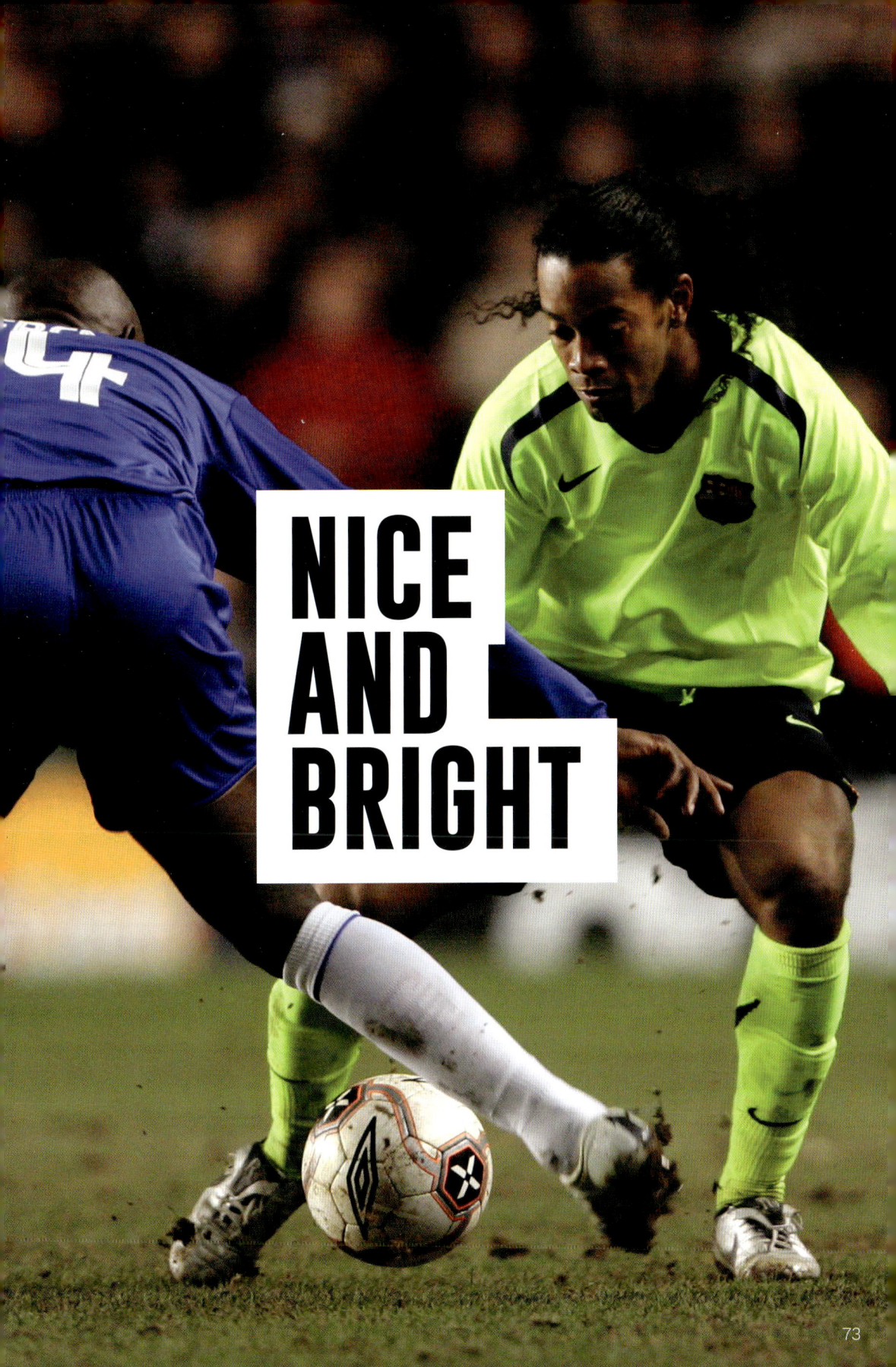

A winner of the trophy as a player with Milan and Ajax, Barcelona boss Frank Rijkaard oversaw more Champions League success in 2005-06 when he brought Europe's top prize back to the Nou Camp for the second time in the club's history.

It was a remarkable campaign for Barca, who also retained the La Liga crown they had won the season before but by a much more substantial margin, taking the title by 12 points after hitting the top spot in November. A year earlier they had won the championship by four points, but the new charge was not all plain sailing; the first seven league games brought four draws and it needed an outstanding 3-0 win at Real Madrid to initially take the top of the table spot.

The club also improved on their previous effort in Europe, having been eliminated by Chelsea in the first knockout round in 2004-05. The sides met again at the same stage, and on this occasion it was Barca that progressed after a win at Stamford Bridge and then a battling draw back at home. There was another England vs. Spain clash the following night too, with Arsenal edging past Real Madrid 1-0 on aggregate having already secured a fine victory in the first leg.

Arsenal and Barcelona had both won their groups, enjoying similar records in which they earned 16 points and only conceded two goals. Barca's ferociousness continued into the quarters and semis, whilst time and time again Brazilian superstar Ronaldinho led the way. He opened the scoring in the second leg of the last eight match against Benfica to kick start a 2-0 win, whilst in the semi-finals it was Ludovic Giuly's first leg strike that made the difference.

Irresistible going forward but ruthless in defence, Barcelona went into the Champions League final as clear favourites against Arsenal despite their own impressive continuation in the competition. The Gunners had overcome Juventus and then Villarreal, where another 1-0 aggregate success had prevented an all-Spanish final.

The Stade de France was the venue for the game in which Arsenal wore their yellow and black away strip, the shirt being a similar design to that of Barcelona's own change option. Sadly though for Arsenal, it was red they saw when goalkeeper Jens Lehmann was dismissed for bringing down Samuel Eto'o. It was the first time a player had been sent off in the final and whilst Arsenal fought bravely the disadvantage eventually told. Leading via Sol Campbell's header shortly before half time, they fell to late replies from Eto'o and Juliano Belletti as Barcelona came through on top.

BARCELONA 2005-06

WINNERS — La Liga
QTR-FINALS — Copa del Rey
WINNERS — UEFA Champions League

FRANK RIJKAARD

SAMUEL ETO'O

EUROPEAN CUP IN NUMBERS

125 GAMES

285 GOALS

MOST APPEARANCES
GIOVANNI VAN BRONCKHORST / CESC FÀBREGAS (13)
Barcelona & Arsenal

TOP SCORER
ANDRIY SHEVCHENKO (9)
AC Milan

MOST GOALS
BARCELONA (24)

MOST CLEAN SHEETS
ARSENAL (10)

25% Liverpool qualified as holders of the competition and four other English clubs entered due to their league placings the season before. A quarter of the Premier League had made it into the 2005-06 competition.

-2 Group C saw Barcelona go through. Bremen finished runners-up albeit level on points with Udinese, who dropped into the UEFA Cup due to a -2 goal difference.

2005-06 UEFA Champions League Final | 17 May 2006, Saint-Denis

BARCELONA 2-1 ARSENAL

S. Eto'o 76'
Belletti 80'

S. Campbell 37

BENFICA 2007-08 AWAY

Looks wise, the 2007-08 Benfica back up kit was experimental to say the least. An unusual salmon pink and graphite colour combination was released, with the sleeves being different colours to one another and white stripes placed across the torso. As for the production, adidas pushed the boat out, using their patented climacool and perforated fabrics, making the shirt up with several different pieces of material that were intricately sewn together. The different logos of PT and TMN, two communications brands that were under the same parent company, were adopted at different points during the campaign, with Benfica wearing a more typical red and white first choice option.

CHANGING IT UP

BENFICA 2007-08 AWAY

Benfica are Portugal's most successful club in Europe, the side having been only the second team to win the European Cup and making a total of seven finals. The last of these appearances was in 1990, although in more recent times they have reached two UEFA Europa League finals and continue to be a strong opponent in European competition.

2007-08, however, was not a vintage season for them in the Champions League. After looking good against Copenhagen in the third qualifying round they were hopeful of progressing from Group D but defeats in the first two games, including a surprise home loss to Shakhtar Donetsk, had the side on the back foot. A win over Celtic, draw against Milan and then a win in the final match in Ukraine did salvage a transfer into the UEFA Cup, but after being parachuted into the Round of 32 and winning 3-2 on aggregate over FC Nürnberg two more defeats soon followed, this time to Getafe.

None of the teams moving on from Group D had much joy in fact, with both Milan and Celtic being knocked out in the Champions League round of 16. The quarter-finals included all four English sides, with two of them making it to the final – Manchester United seeing off Chelsea in Russia following a 1-1 draw after extra time that was concluded on penalties. United stopper Edwin van der Sar saved from Nicolas Anelka as the team won the shoot-out 6-5, the Red Devils having originally led through Cristiano Ronaldo's header before being pegged back by Frank Lampard's finish from inside the penalty area.

By that point Benfica could only watch on in envy, knowing that the following season they wouldn't even be in the Champions League after finishing the season fourth in the Primeira Liga. It seemed harsh having only lost four league games, which was three less than the teams in second and third, but a series of draws stifled progress and they finished a humbling 23 points behind champions Porto.

Highlights did include a 6-1 home win over Boavista and the win over Shakhtar but a series of managerial changes pointed towards this being a season of transition. Perennial winners Benfica were used to success but had now gone three seasons without a trophy, losing this time in the fourth round of the inaugural League Cup and then the semi-finals of the Taça de Portugal.

BENFICA 2007-08

4TH PLACE — Primeira Liga
SEMI-FINALS — Taça de Portugal
4TH ROUND — Taça da Liga
GROUP STAGE — UEFA Champions League

FERNANDO SANTOS
(until August 2007), then José Antonio Camacho (until March 2008), and then Fernando Chalana (caretaker)

ÓSCAR CARDOZO

EUROPEAN CUP IN NUMBERS

125 GAMES
330 GOALS

MOST APPEARANCES
JOE COLE / CLAUDE MAKÉLÉLÉ (13) Chelsea

TOP SCORER
CRISTIANO RONALDO (8) Manchester United

MOST GOALS
LIVERPOOL (29)

MOST CLEAN SHEETS
MANCHESTER UNITED (8)

80 With just ten minutes left, Fenerbahce scored in their round of 16 second leg against Sevilla, bringing the tie back all square at 5-5, then progressing on penalties.

2000 This is roughly how many miles United fans travelling from Manchester would have had to drive to see the game in Russia. Chelsea fans were slightly closer with 1800 miles one way.

2007-08 UEFA Champions League Group D | 4 December 2007, Donetsk

SHAKHTAR DONETSK 1-2 BENFICA

C. Lucarelli 30' (pen)   O. Cardozo 6', 22'

INTER MILAN 2009-10 HOME

Inter Milan returned to the top of the European tree after 40 years, and their kit had a definite retro feel. Featuring a round neck and black central stripe, Nike went with a tailored approach reminiscent of Inter's glory years of the mid-1960s when they won the league three times and twice became European Cup winners. There were further touches to mark their heritage including a small Milan flag on the inside collar and a side tag celebrating the 100th anniversary of their first Serie A success. Tyre manufacturers Pirelli stretched across the chest now as well, and there was another twist – they wore white socks in the Champions League final instead of their preferred black, thus avoiding a clash with Bayern Munich.

GOING OLD SCHOOL

INTER MILAN 2009-10 HOME

Magnificent Inter Milan completed a clean sweep of major honours, earning themselves a fifth successive scudetto, beating Roma in the final of the Coppa Italia and then rounding it off with the big one… the Champions League.

It remains the most successful season in the club's history, yet none of it was a forgone conclusion. After a number of draws in the league, the title went down to the last game with a crucial 1-0 win over Siena that came 11 days after another tight victory in the cup final. To make the task even harder that match had been staged at the home of opponents Roma, but Diego Milito popped up in both fixtures to score the winners.

The Argentina international was equally influential in the Champions League during what was his first season at Inter. After drawing their first three group games, Milito's late equaliser against Dynamo Kyiv prompted a last gasp victory. Although the side then lost to Barcelona, a vital win over Rubin Kazan meant they squeezed through to a knockout tie with Chelsea. Milito opened the scoring moments into the first leg to send Inter on their way to a 3-1 aggregate passage in that one, and he was then on target again in the quarter-final first leg win against CSKA Moscow.

This time Inter won 2-0 on aggregate and whilst there were some tense moments in the semi-final second leg at holders Barcelona, José Mourinho's men had done enough to go through over the two games. It meant a return trip to Spain for the final in Madrid, where they would be facing a fully charged Bayern Munich team that were also gunning for a triple haul having already won their domestic league and cup with comparative ease.

The main event was held on a Saturday for the first time and Inter were returning after a long absence, having not reached the final since losing to Ajax in 1972. Bayern had made seven appearances since then, winning four of them, and had finished above them in Group B of the 2006-07 competition, but they faced a side that oozed confidence and had little answer for the movement of Milito.

With just over half an hour gone the striker put his team ahead with a cool finish, before another goal from the Argentine hitman with just 20 minutes to go. Milito's brace had given Milan their first European Cup in 45 years, and Mourinho his second Champions League title.

INTER MILAN 2009-10

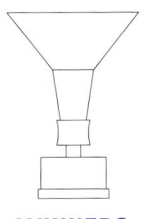
WINNERS
Serie A

WINNERS
Coppa Italia

WINNERS
UEFA Champions League

👤 **JOSÉ MOURINHO**

⚽ **DIEGO MILITO**

EUROPEAN CUP IN NUMBERS

125 GAMES

320 GOALS

MOST APPEARANCES
MAICON (13)
Inter Milan

TOP SCORER
LIONEL MESSI (8)
Barcelona

MOST GOALS
MANCHESTER UNITED (21)

MOST CLEAN SHEETS
INTER MILAN (6)

2 Beaten once in the group stages and in their semi-final second leg, winners Inter could afford to lose twice during the competition and still earn glory.

211 Both sides had been awarded the same number of free kicks in the 2009-10 tournament. Inter however received ten more cards and gave away 196 fouls to Bayern's 169.

2009-10 UEFA Champions League Final | 22 May 2010, Madrid

BAYERN MUNICH 0-2 INTER MILAN

D. Milito 35', 70'

CHELSEA 2011-12 HOME

By the 2010s football shirts had long since become an essential fashion item for supporters. For the players though, the science of kit design had moved on too, with moisture wicking materials now common at the highest level and ergonomic factors being considered. Chelsea won their first Champions League wearing a two tone blue shirt that utilised adidas' TECHFIT technology to aid movement, the slim line tops displaying white patches on the shoulders that matched the makers logo and that of club sponsor Samsung. When a change was needed on the road, they had a black away kit with blue screen print patterning and a white third choice that had contrasting bands along the upper section to choose from.

PERFORMING NEW MATERIAL

CHELSEA 2011-12 HOME

In 2012 Chelsea took the Champions League after a series of near misses. Having qualified for the competition for the past eight seasons, the London outfit had reached four semi-finals and a final in that period, but despite a particularly daunting task they ensured that this time they went the whole way.

A busy summer transfer window under new manager André Villas-Boas preceded the campaign and they came through a tricky looking group with victories over Bayer Leverkusen, Genk and then Valencia in the final fixture to ensure top spot. Progress then looked to have stalled with a damaging round of 16 first leg loss at Napoli but, with Villas-Boas being replaced by his assistant and former Chelsea player Roberto Di Matteo in the interim, the side stormed back in the second game to win 4-1 on the night and 5-4 overall.

A quarter-final double over Benfica then led to a grudge match with Barcelona, who had been drawn against Chelsea three times before in recent seasons including a highly contentious tie at the same stage in 2009 where they were denied several penalty appeals. Barca went on to win the Champions League that season, but this time it was different – Chelsea went through in extraordinary style when despite being down to ten men, Fernando Torres scored in second leg added on time to give them a 3-2 aggregate win.

It was captain John Terry that had been sent off in the Nou Camp, meaning he was suspended for the final alongside three other senior members of the squad, which only made things worse given that the game was already due to be hosted in the home ground of opponents Bayern. The Germans looked set to make the most of that advantage too when Thomas Müller scored with less than ten minutes left, but Didier Drogba soon responded.

That was the last of the open play goals, but the Blues' favourite, who had scored the first goal of the semi-final, then came up with an even more important effort. Chelsea had lost the 2008 Champions League on penalties, and this was the first shoot-out in the final since then. Goalkeeper Petr Čech stood out in all white and made two excellent stops to go with an earlier penalty stop in extra time, allowing the Ivorian to nonchalantly tuck away the winner.

It was an impressive feat given the disruption of changing managers, and whilst Di Matteo had been unable to catch up those ahead in the league, a win over Liverpool in the FA Cup two weeks earlier meant this was now a remarkable double.

CHELSEA 2011-12

6TH PLACE
Premier League

WINNERS
English FA Cup

QTR-FINALS
English League Cup

WINNERS
UEFA Champions League

ANDRÉ VILLAS-BOAS
(until March 2012), then Roberto Di Matteo (caretaker)

FRANK LAMPARD
⚽⚽⚽⚽⚽⚽⚽⚽⚽⚽⚽⚽⚽⚽⚽

EUROPEAN CUP IN NUMBERS

125 GAMES

345 GOALS

MOST APPEARANCES
JÉRÔME BOATENG / PETR ČECH (13)
Bayern Munich & Chelsea

TOP SCORER
LIONEL MESSI (14)
Barcelona

MOST GOALS
BARCELONA/REAL MADRID (35)

MOST CLEAN SHEETS
REAL MADRID (6)

33 The speed in kilometres per hour Chelsea's Ramires was said to have reached according to UEFA – the fastest in the competition that season. Franck Ribéry was next on the list after hitting 32 km/h.

94 Real Madrid's Pepe made the most 'recoveries' during the 2011-12 tournament. He won the ball back nearly 100 times for his side.

2011-12 UEFA Champions League Final | 19 May 2012, Munich

BAYERN MUNICH 1-1 CHELSEA

T. Müller 83' **(3-4 PENS)** D. Drogba 88'

BAYERN MUNICH 2012-13 HOME

The 2013 Champions League final wasn't just a clash of the two biggest clubs in Germany – it was also a clash of the two biggest kit manufacturers from the country too. The origin stories and rivalry between adidas and PUMA are well known, and this time it was the former that came out on top, with their long running association with winners Bayern Munich continuing to bear fruit. They released several kits for 2012-13, although the one worn in the final was mainly used the following season. Before that, a standard burgundy and gold home strip, white change strip and 'Champions League' black ensemble had all been seen in European fixtures. At Wembley, Bayern wore a simple red outfit with smart white trim and subtle Bavarian lozenge micro shadowing.

BAYERN MUNICH 2012-13 HOME

Driven on by the pain of losing the Champions League in their own back yard the season before, Bayern Munich were in no mood to let the prize slip from their grasp again in 2012-13. Their conquerors Chelsea became the first holders not to get out of the group stage, and without the possibility of a revenge match Bayern instead ploughed on through to take on domestic rivals Borussia Dortmund in the final, which ironically enough was held in Chelsea's home city of London.

The Bavarians used a designated Champions League kit for a lot of their games and it ensured they would not forget their earlier defeat, depicting as it did the illuminated outer skin of their Allianz Arena stadium within the micro detailing. The black and silver design and the red kit they introduced for the final both carried the logo of their sponsors Deutsche Telekom, with the shirts worn in the final also including the club motto 'Mia san Mia', which was embossed below the collars on the back, although replica versions instead read 'Bayern Munich'.

Bayern had to knuckle down to get past Arsenal on away goals in the first knockout stage after topping their group, and making light work of Lille and BATE Borisov at home. A win and a draw meant they finished above Valencia due to a superior head-to-head record, but whilst the Spaniards were then eliminated Bayern kept improving. In the quarters they swept aside Juventus with a pair of 2-0 wins, that was relatively close in comparison to the 7-0 demolition of Barcelona that came afterwards.

Dortmund, meanwhile, had also disposed of a European giant when they beat Real Madrid over two legs but, in being runners-up to Bayern in the Bundesliga, they had finished a whopping 25 points behind their dominant champions. The gap in Champions League prize money was also stark, with the losing finalists set to net €4 million less than the €10.5 million on offer for the winners, but the match itself proved to be a close run thing.

Bayern were German Cup winners that season and, with a string of new records set on the domestic front, had beaten Dortmund in both the DFB-Pokal and Super Cup earlier in the campaign but both league games had finished level. The final itself was equally close, with only Arjen Robben's late deft touch separating the sides after İlkay Gündoğan's penalty had cancelled out Mario Mandžukić's opener.

BAYERN MUNICH 2012-13

WINNERS
Bundesliga

WINNERS
DFB-Pokal

WINNERS
UEFA Champions League

 **JUPP HEYNCKES**

⚽ **THOMAS MÜLLER**
⚽⚽⚽⚽⚽⚽⚽⚽⚽⚽⚽⚽⚽⚽⚽⚽⚽⚽

EUROPEAN CUP IN NUMBERS

125 GAMES

MOST APPEARANCES
MANUEL NEUER (13)
Bayern Munich

TOP SCORER
CRISTIANO RONALDO (12)
Real Madrid

368 GOALS

MOST GOALS
BAYERN MUNICH (31)

MOST CLEAN SHEETS
BAYERN MUNICH (5)

11 This was the tenth time Bayern Munich had reached the final and they have won it once more since then too, meaning that they are joint second with AC Milan for the most finals competed in.

6 Cristiano Ronaldo was the tournament's top scorer, and joint top scorer for six consecutive seasons.

2012-13 UEFA Champions League Final | 25 May 2013, London

B. DORTMUND 1-2 BAYERN MUNICH

İ. Gündoğan 68'

Mario Mandžukić 60'
Robben 89'

ATLETICO MADRID 2015-16 HOME

Whilst there were some bespoke variations, Nike's provision for Atletico Madrid was in keeping with their 2015-16 teamwear range. They included four different goalkeeper choices and an elegant navy change strip, whilst the first choice kit reflected their traditional colours – although the white stripes were only seen on the front of a red base shirt that had additional blue trim. The player issues boasted heat sealed ventilation holes, meshed fabric backs and printed wash labels for reduced irritation, whilst the tops also had an internal symbol to commemorate the tenth anniversary of what had been their first title win in two decades. Atletico had enjoyed a memorable arrangement with Columbia Pictures a decade earlier that had seen several blockbuster titles adorn their strips, but by the 2016 Champions League final online trading platform Plus500 were onboard.

ATLETICO MADRID 2015-16 HOME

This wasn't a case of third time lucky for Atletico Madrid, who in 2016 lost the Champions League final having already been beaten in their previous two. They are the only side in competition history to lose three or more without ever having won one, and to make matters worse the last two were against local rivals Real Madrid.

What shouldn't be forgotten though is that just getting that far was an achievement in itself, and that whilst the top prize has alluded them, they do still have a good record. Cup Winners' Cup victors in 1962, they have also won the UEFA Europa League three times.

Manager Diego Simeone delivered two of these as well as several considerable accomplishments domestically. He was credited too with plotting Atletico's course to the 2016 final, starting with a composed win at the home of Galatasaray and whilst they then lost at home to Benfica and could only draw away to Astana, who had just become the first club from Kazakhstan to reach that stage, they were still comfortable winners of their group.

This brought PSV Eindhoven to the capital, where after two edgy goalless draws and an additional period of extra time the tie had to be settled by penalties. There was still little to split the two teams, but after eventually going through 8-7 Atletico then had to face up to holders Barcelona. Unfazed, however, by a 2-1 first leg deficit and the absence of his talismanic partner Fernando Torres through suspension, star forward Antoine Griezmann scored twice as his team roared back at a frenzied Vicente Calderon Stadium.

The home crowd then enjoyed a semi-final first leg win over Bayern Munich before Griezmann's vital strike in the return leg resulted in an away goals progression to the final at the San Siro. Atletico had already beaten Real in the league and finished just two points behind them in the table, and after seeing them pull away in extra time of the 2014 final to win 4-1 this occasion proved a closer run thing.

There was no need for the newly introduced goal-line technology when Sergio Ramos put Real ahead, although replays later suggested that, had VAR been in place, it would have been disallowed for offside. There was still time for Atletico to respond however, and despite Griezmann missing a penalty Yannick Carrasco converted from close range to bring extra time. A winner couldn't be found though, so it went down to spot kicks again – Juanfran, who had created the leveller, being the one to miss his penalty before Cristiano Ronaldo sealed the deal.

ATLETICO MADRID 2015-16

3RD PLACE
La Liga

QTR-FINALS
Copa del Rey

RUNNERS-UP
UEFA Champions League

 DIEGO SIMEONE

⚽ **ANTOINE GRIEZMANN**

EUROPEAN CUP IN NUMBERS

125 GAMES

347 GOALS

MOST APPEARANCES
JAN OBLAK / GABI (13)
Atletico Madrid

TOP SCORER
CRISTIANO RONALDO (16) Real Madrid

MOST GOALS
BAYERN MUNICH (30)

MOST CLEAN SHEETS
REAL MADRID (10)

80 Winners Real Madrid led the way in terms of clean sheets, but Manchester City made the most successful tackles whilst attempting to halt their opponents' progress.

86.8 Toni Kroos played more than 1000 passes during the tournament in 2015-16 as he helped drive Real Madrid to the trophy. Of these, 952 were completed – meaning a phenomenal success rate of 86.8%.

2015-16 UEFA Champions League Final | 28 May 2016, Milan

REAL MADRID 1-1 ATLETICO MADRID
S. Ramos 15' **(5-3 PENS)** Y. Carrasco 79'

FEYENOORD 2017-18 HOME

This wasn't a vintage season for Feyenoord in Europe, who at least looked good in their kits even when the results didn't quite match. With an impressive record in past competitions, they had worn their classic red and white half and half shirts in the finals when winning the 1970 European Cup and 2002 UEFA Cup, as well as in the second leg of their 1974 UEFA cup success, and this combination was again in use. Adidas halves with alternating sleeves were coupled with black shorts and socks, with the away option being a love it or hate it green and black pattern where the 'three stripes' ran down the sides of the body instead of the shoulders and sleeves. It was a suitable colour choice for sponsors Qurrent, a green energy supplier whose presence on the tops was reduced in size during Champions League outings.

FAMOUS HALVED SHIRTS

FEYENOORD 2017-18 HOME

Feyenoord started and ended their season with silverware; it was some of the games in between that proved the problem. Winning the Johan Cruyff Shield against Vitesse to kick 2017-18 off instigated a strong start to the season that saw Giovanni van Bronckhorst's side top the early table but, by the time of the KNVB Cup final in late April, the title charge had died off and the side had tumbled out of the Champions League.

The Dutch Cup final was played, as per tradition, in Rotterdam and whilst Feyenoord were technically the away side against AZ Alkmaar they still won the game 3-0. All of their five previous ties that season had been home draws as well incidentally, meaning they were played at the same venue as the 2002 UEFA Cup final – which was also won by Rotterdam.

That victory was one of three European trophies won during the club's history but hopes of more continental glory in this campaign were quickly put out. As reigning Eredivisie Champions they went straight into the group stages, but lost their opening match 4-0 at home to Manchester City and struggled to bounce back.

The next four games were all lost as well, but whilst the side finished bottom of Group F they did at least sign off in style with victory over Napoli. Trailing to an early effort from Piotr Zieliński, 'De Stadionclub' were determined to give their fans something positive and, after levelling through Nicolai Jørgensen, clawed back further pride thanks to Jeremiah St. Juste's injury time winner.

The two sides to progress in the tournament from their group, City and Shakhtar Donetsk, both did not reach the semi-finals. Those games were instead contested by Bayern Munich and Real Madrid, and Liverpool and Roma as the major leagues continued to dominate – this being the 14th year in a row where the finalists came from one of those countries and the fifth with at least one Spanish club taking part.

This time it was Real Madrid, who went on to win the competition for the third time running. Not since Milan in 1990 had any side managed to secure back-to-back triumphs, but Real emphasised their dominance in Kyiv with a strong display to overcome Liverpool 3-1. The two teams had met in the 1981 European Cup final when the English were winners, but now Real were well and truly in charge.

FEYENOORD 2017-18

4TH PLACE
Eredivisie

WINNERS
KNVB Cup

GROUP STAGE
UEFA Champions League

 **GIOVANNI VAN BRONCKHORST**

⚽ **STEVEN BERGHUIS**

EUROPEAN CUP IN NUMBERS

125 GAMES

401 GOALS

MOST APPEARANCES
CRISTIANO RONALDO / MOHAMED SALAH (13) Real Madrid & Liverpool

TOP SCORER
CRISTIANO RONALDO (15) Real Madrid

MOST GOALS
LIVERPOOL (41)

MOST CLEAN SHEETS
LIVERPOOL/BARCELONA (6)

9 The third qualifying round split into two subsections — Champions route for league winners from underperforming nations and League route for those finishing high within stronger leagues. In the League route, Steaua Bucharest won 6-3 on aggregate over Viktoria Plzeň.

112 Real Madrid left it late in their quarter-final second leg with Bayern; with goals coming in the 105th, 110th and 112th minutes.

2017-18   UEFA Champions League Group F | 6 December 2017, Rotterdam

FEYENOORD 2-1 NAPOLI

N. Jørgensen 33'   P. Zieliński 2'
J. St. Juste 90+1'

PSV EINDHOVEN 2018-19 HOME

The big three in the Netherlands all wear combinations of red and white, with Eindhoven's home design for the 2018-19 season leaning heavily on the former with the shirts incorporating an almost entirely red back, and red raglan sleeves. Bringing together historical elements and modern touches, a small symbol on the back of the shirt depicted a plaque that had been installed to celebrate the club's centenary earlier in the decade, whilst new melange effect fibres and Umbro double diamond cuff detailing brought things up to date. The biggest adaption had come two years earlier however, when utility company Energiedirect had replaced Philips as main sponsor – the club having originally been a works team for employees of the consumer goods factory.

PSV EINDHOVEN 2018-19 HOME

Dutch clubs had been struggling in the Champions League for more than a decade when PSV Eindhoven returned in 2018 as newly crowned Eredivisie holders. In 2006-07 they had been the last club from the Netherlands to reach the quarter-finals and whilst that sequence was about to be broken at last, it was not by themselves.

Poor coefficient numbers meant that even as league winners PSV would have to take part in the qualifying stages, coming in at the play-off round as part of the 'Champions Path'. In the first leg they travelled to Belarus to play BATE Borisov, and after leaving with a 3-2 win they made sure with a 3-0 victory at the Philips Stadion. It was a thoroughly professional display and at that point the pundits were expecting more, but the following day's draw for the group stage did them no favours.

Borisov had been one of the tougher opponents PSV could have faced in the play-offs and they were then dumped into a veritable group of death. The team did well to force a late draw to Tottenham Hotspur and take a point off Inter in the final game, but with Barcelona to contend with they finished bottom without a win.

The team had competed well enough but then had to endure rivals Ajax's headline-making progress to the semis. PSV had won the trophy in 1988 when they beat Benfica on penalties, coming ten years after they had captured the UEFA Cup, but the Amsterdam side can boast the Netherlands' best record in European football. Even though they started even further back in the second qualifying round, they almost reached another final after eliminating both Real Madrid and Juventus.

They were attention grabbing results but after making the last four, Ajax bowed out following a sensational contest with PSV's earlier opponents Tottenham. Seemingly out when three down on aggregate with little more than half an hour of the second leg left, Spurs fought back to win on away goals following Lucas Moura's intervention deep into added time. It was a brilliant game and served as the perfect accompaniment to an equally breathless match the night before, where Liverpool had recovered from three goals down to oust Barcelona.

The all-English final would struggle to match the previous round for drama, although Liverpool skipper Jordan Henderson was not complaining when he lifted the trophy following a 2-0 win. Three weeks earlier Ajax had made up for their elimination by winning their first title in five years, narrowly pipping PSV.

PSV EINDHOVEN 2018-19

RUNNERS-UP — Eredivisie
2ND ROUND — KNVB Cup
GROUP STAGE — UEFA Champions League

 **MARK VAN BOMMEL**

 **LUUK DE JONG**
⚽⚽⚽⚽⚽⚽⚽⚽⚽⚽⚽⚽⚽⚽⚽⚽⚽⚽⚽⚽⚽⚽⚽⚽⚽⚽

EUROPEAN CUP IN NUMBERS

125 GAMES
366 GOALS

MOST APPEARANCES
ALISSON / SADIO MANÉ (13) Liverpool

TOP SCORER
LIONEL MESSI (12) Barcelona

MOST GOALS
MANCHESTER CITY (30)

MOST CLEAN SHEETS
LIVERPOOL/BARCELONA (6)

615 The number of times 2018-19 winners Liverpool mounted an attack during the competition. Their opponents in the final, Tottenham Hotspur, forced the most corners, winning 80 in total.

2.93 There was a goal for every 31 minutes of Champions League play during the tournament, with an average per game of just under three.

2018-19 UEFA Champions League Play-Off Round | 29 August 2018, Eindhoven

PSV EINDHOVEN 3-0 BATE BORISOV

S. Bergwijn 14',
L. De Jong 36', H. Lozano 62'

PARIS SAINT-GERMAIN 2019-20 HOME

The worldwide COVID-19 pandemic affected almost every aspect of life during 2020, even football kits. Champions League finalists Paris Saint-Germain introduced a plethora of 'specials' carrying messages of goodwill or supporting those dealing with the virus and come the final itself wore their 'caregiver tribute' edition with the word 'Merci' on the chest and a small tricolore on the left sleeve. Some change and goalkeeper strips carried Nike's Jumpman logo instead of the usual Swoosh, with the home effort being based on the renowned Daniel Hechter navy, white and red vision first implemented in 1973. Accommodation and hospitality company Accor's customer rewards programme took centre stage as sponsors, with PSG's look completed with a small collar insert, seen on most Nike shirts that season, upon which the word Paris was lightly flocked.

With the French season being truncated by worldwide events, Paris Saint-Germain were awarded the Ligue 1 title on a points per game basis. That was in April and at the end of July, when fixtures were able to be staged again, the club completed a domestic treble by beating Saint-Etienne in the French Cup and then Lyon, on penalties, in the French League Cup.

Restrictions meant that what would have usually been sell out occasions were attended by only a few thousand. Just having the games take place was providing many more supporters with a much needed break from reality, and PSG were giving them some cheer. They came within a fraction of winning a first Champions League too, after it was decided that the final stages should be restructured and played in Portugal as one-off ties over the course of 11 days in August.

To get that far, PSG had topped Group A with five wins, and a 2-2 draw at Real Madrid whom they had swatted aside 3-0 already in their first game. The team then went onto a round of 16 match up with Borussia Dortmund that was part of the first set of fixtures, meaning it was completed before the decision to postpone games in the face of increasing concerns about the spread of covid.

Some sides had to wait for their second legs to be rescheduled, but PSG had already overturned a 2-1 first leg deficit when Neymar and Juan Bernat scored to put them through 3-2 on aggregate. Then came a long wait whilst the next steps were decided, with Thomas Tuchel's team eventually going up against Atalanta in Lisbon. With the match slipping away, goals in the 90th minute and added on time got them out of jail, and the semi was a much more controlled affair in which RB Leipzig were beaten 3-0.

That brought about a clash with another German side, with Bayern Munich making their 11th appearance in the final having earlier thrashed Barcelona 8-2. PSG's record, meanwhile, did not quite stack up – although they had often been a big draw in Europe all they had to show for it was the 1995-96 Cup Winners' Cup, and after losing a close encounter 1-0 thanks to Kingsley Coman's second half header, they were left to wonder when their time would come in the Champions League.

To make matters worse, Coman was a Paris native and former PSG player, but given the wider context the result didn't seem to matter quite as much.

PARIS SAINT-GERMAIN 2019-20

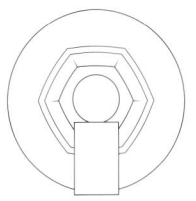
WINNERS
Ligue 1

WINNERS
Coupe de France

WINNERS
Coupe de la Ligue

RUNNERS-UP
UEFA Champions League

 **THOMAS TUCHEL**
⚽ **KYLIAN MBAPPÉ**
⚽⚽⚽⚽⚽⚽⚽⚽⚽⚽
⚽⚽⚽⚽⚽⚽⚽⚽⚽⚽
⚽⚽⚽⚽⚽

EUROPEAN CUP IN NUMBERS

119 GAMES

386 GOALS

MOST APPEARANCES
JOSHUA KIMMICH (11)
Bayern Munich

TOP SCORER
ROBERT LEWANDOWSKI (15) Bayern Munich

MOST GOALS
BAYERN MUNICH (43)

MOST CLEAN SHEETS
PARIS SAINT-GERMAIN (7)

-6 The pandemic meant a temporary stop was put on the competition. The quarter and semi-finals being decided via one off matches and the tournament concluding three months later than planned, with six fewer games.

100 Winners Bayern Munich were faultless throughout the 2019-20 Champions League, winning all 11 of their fixtures, achieving a perfect 100 per cent record.

2019-20 UEFA Champions League Final | 23 August 2020, Lisbon

PSG 0-1 BAYERN MUNICH

K. Coman 59'

SHERIFF TIRASPOL 2021-22 HOME

Nicknamed the Zholto-chornyye (yellow-blacks), Moldova's most successful club Sheriff Tiraspol, unsurprisingly, nearly always play in one of the two colours – if not both. In some cases over recent seasons their home and away kits were the same design as each other with just the main colour and trims switched around, although in 2021-22 a white detailing was retained and just the main colours were alternated. This was the season when Sheriff came to prominence after a shock victory against Real Madrid, winning in Spain whilst wearing uncluttered all-black adidas kits with monochrome club crests and fade pattern sleeves but little else in the way of features. It was a simple effort based on a template with the lack of a sponsor giving it an old school feel.

SHERIFF TIRASPOL 2021-22 HOME

The Champions League has provided the stage for some of the biggest clubs on the planet to clash over the years, but it has also seen a whole host of other teams try and achieve their goals and make an impression. That was never clearer than in 2021, when Sheriff Tiraspol shocked the most successful club in the competition's history in their own back yard.

Beating Real Madrid 2-1 with a late winner from Sébastien Thill propelled Sheriff into the limelight, but the first Moldovan side to ever reach the group stages already had a wealth of European experience and had enjoyed multiple successes in their homeland, with the upset in Spain being the culmination of a whole lot of hard work.

Winners of the previous six Divizia Națională (now Super Liga) titles, the club first qualified for Europe in 1999 and had done so every year since. Cutting their teeth in preliminary rounds and Europa League matches, their journey continued with a mammoth schedule in 2021-22 that started in the first qualifying round and then ended back in the Europa League – the side playing 16 European games in total when their league programme only totalled 28.

Things kicked off with a win in Albania as Teuta were seen off 5-0 on aggregate. Armenia was next on the itinerary as Alashkert were disposed of and then came two relatively big guns – Red Star Belgrade and Dinamo Zagreb. Neither side were able to slow Sheriff's progress and whilst they failed to get out of Group D they weren't just there to make up the numbers either, scoring in both games against Inter Milan as well as pulling off their momentous Madrid victory.

A home win over Shakhtar Donetsk was also secured, as was a draw against the same opposition in the final game, and that meant a transfer into the knockout round play-off of UEFA's secondary competition. There they faced Braga, and whilst the adventure came to an end for another season Sheriff still pushed all the way – only going down on penalties after two matches and a period of extra time.

Braga got as far as the quarter-finals of the Europa League, whereas Real Madrid recovered from their Sherriff ordeal in the best way possible. By going on to beat Paris Saint-Germain, Chelsea, Manchester City and then Liverpool in the final they tightened their grip on the tournament, winning the trophy for the 14th time and keeping them well ahead of the next best club, Milan, on seven.

SHERIFF TIRASPOL 2021-22

WINNERS
Divizia Națională

WINNERS
Moldovan Cup

GROUP STAGE
UEFA Champions League

 YURIY VERNYDUB
(until February 2022), then Dmytro Kara-Mustafa

⚽ **ADAMA TRAORÉ**

EUROPEAN CUP IN NUMBERS

125 GAMES

MOST APPEARANCES
LUKA MODRIĆ (13)
Real Madrid

TOP SCORER
KARIM BENZEMA (15)
Real Madrid

380 GOALS

MOST GOALS
BAYERN MUNICH (31)

MOST CLEAN SHEETS
CHELSEA (5)

80 The number of teams taking part in the competition including qualifying stages, coming from a total of 54 different countries. When the European Cup started in 1955 there were 16 entrants.

3 The 2021-22 round of 16 draw saw a technical fault, with teams that couldn't face each other at that stage being incorrectly paired. The draw was redone three hours later.

2020-21 UEFA Champions League Group D | 28 September 2021, Madrid

REAL MADRID 1-2 SHERIFF

K. Benzema 65' (pen)

J. Yakhshiboev 25'
S. Thill 90'

THE CHAMPIONS LEAGUE

CLASSIC KITS

Written by Andrew Smithson
Designed by Daniel Brawn

ASPEN BOOKS

© 2023. Published by Aspen Books, an imprint of Pillar Box Red Publishing Ltd. Printed in India.

This is an independent publication. It has no connection with any of the football clubs featured or with any organisation or individual connected in any way whatsoever with the football clubs or with the UEFA Champions League.

Any quotes within this publication which are attributed to anyone connected to the tournament or football clubs have been sourced from other publications or from the internet and, as such, are a matter of public record.

Whilst every effort has been made to ensure the accuracy of information within this publication, the publisher shall have no liability to any person or entity with respect to any inaccuracy, misleading information, loss or damage caused directly or indirectly by the information contained within this book.

The views expressed are solely those of the author and do not reflect the opinions of Aspen Books. All rights reserved.

ISBN: 978-1-914536-72-4

Images © Alamy